Angry Parents No More!

Practical strategies and exercises to understand your anger, manage your emotions and become a more emotionally intelligent parent

HATTIE ELLEDGE

D1372241

SPECIAL BONUS!

Want This Bonus Book for FREE?

Get FREE, unlimited access to it and all of my new books by joining the Fan Base!

Scan me!

Contents

Introduction

I remember being roused out of bed, pulled deep from slumber and physically dragged by the arm to the kitchen, my mother vehemently screaming at me about an improperly cleaned pot that had the audacity to sit on the washed side of the sink drain. The tirade of her words slapped me about as no hands could do, the octave at which she spat them at me hurt my eardrums, and the fact I could make no rebuttal to tell her my sister had washed up seemed incredibly unjust. Standing there in my pajamas, only half awake, being lambasted by this fury of a woman for not doing something exactly to her liking, I remember thinking how horrid her anger was and how scary she became. I was twelve years old.

This is my first memory of dealing with parental anger - on the receiving end of it. Throughout my childhood, I became accustomed to this response whenever my mother was unhappy about pretty much anything. My siblings and I called it poking the bear, and we tried our level best never to poke the bear. But, of course, we did. We were children, and children always make mistakes and do things that will inevitably annoy their parents in one way or another. The thing is, everybody out there makes mistakes, children and adults alike, a fact I am well aware of these days because I am now a parent, and I make just as many mistakes as my child does. That was one of my greatest fears when I had a little one of my own, the idea that one day I would subject my offspring to what I had gone through with my mother. I vowed I would never be like that.

Instead, I would be calm and patient with my little lamb, at every turn, in every instance, no matter what they did… but then life happens. They doodle all over your friend's living room wall with the lipstick they pulled from your purse, emulating a mural of the breadth and magnitude even Diego Rivera could admire. In a split second, you feel yourself morphing from a normal human being into a seething banshee. Ask any parent because we have all been there. Growing up in that toxic environment, I was overtly aware of it and felt I might be twice as prone to reproduce this behavior if I did not make a concerted effort to stop the cycle of anger as a knee jerk response. This is what I had learned as "appropriate" behavior, even though it is anything but. I studied psychology and child psychology in university to see what sort of negative repercussions came of being subjected to dose after dose of parental anger, for the child as well as for the adult. Low and behold, and not surprisingly, there are negative effects for all parties involved.

When I became a parent, I knew I had to create and maintain a new type of parenting style, not the one filled with yelling and screaming, but something that was healthy for both me and my little one. I also knew I would have to train myself not to go directly to anger, like my mother did, like I found myself prone to do, even when I knew it was hurtful and not at all helpful to anyone involved. The first time I yelled at my child and saw their faces and their tears, I was instantly transported to my 12-year-old self, and I was ashamed, angry, and disappointed that I could behave in this manner towards someone I claimed to love. This was the response and the pattern I was accustomed to, but it was not one I was willing to continue. It takes time to break a cycle, to press pause or stop on a bad habit, but it can be done with a bit of self-awareness, education, and retraining. We all have setbacks! Even as I write this book, at the end of a stressful day, I have had to apologize for getting snippy, but acknowledgement and apologies are two things I never got as a child from my own parents, so I feel like I am at least progressing down the right path, even if it is something I don't think any of us can get right 100% of the time.

Within this book we will look at the root and causes of anger, what it is, where this emotion comes from, the dangers and the values it contains, and how to manage its many forms. We will examine how this strong sentiment flows through us, and we will discuss ways to deal with it, dissipate it, and disavow that emotion as our go-to response for the more difficult and trying situations we face every day as parents. Psychologically, we will talk about the issues it causes in our children and in ourselves, and we will discuss how to deal with any traumas that have arisen or might arise in the future. Various options in parenting styles will be explored, so you can find what works best for your family, because one thing is sure, there is no one right solution for everyone. Helping you improve your day-to-day interactions and reactions, this text will go through healthier ways to communicate and offer you a plethora of positive parenting tips.

Nobody is born a perfect parent, and there is no such thing as the perfect parent. Wipe that notion from your mind right now! We can, however, be great parents with children that love us and do not fear us or our anger. We are open parents that keep the lines of communication with our children on a happy, healthy, and positive track. I was always so afraid to speak to my mother about anything, and this is something no child should have to live with.

Acknowledging that we need to upgrade our anger management is a great step on the road to improvement, and this book will help you down that path to becoming a content, calmer caregiver by giving you detailed instructions on how to create and maintain your own routine of strategies and exercises to improve your overall parenting, leaving you with a happier family. You will be able to continue your role as a parent in a more thoughtful and loving way, one which contains far less reaction and much more patience and understanding. That's what we all really want. This might be a lengthy, ongoing process, but it is one you have already started upon just by picking up this book.

Chapter One
Understanding Parental Anger

What is Anger & Does it Have a Purpose?

When the kids forget to clean their rooms or walk the dog or put away the dishes, our typical response as a parent is to get angry. According to the Oxford Dictionary, anger is defined as, "a strong feeling of annoyance, displeasure, or hostility." The word is both a noun, a thing, and a verb, an action. While raising children, it is definitely something you feel and an action you take almost on a daily basis! Anger is a basic human emotion, but how angry we become depends on each of us as a unique individual and how we respond to outside stimuli (of which our children top the list). Getting upset is a completely normal response, and "anger only becomes a problem when it's excessively displayed and begins to affect your daily functioning and the way you relate with people" (Daniel B. Block MD, What Is Anger?). If, under very little provocation, you react with a bout of uncontrollable temper, this is when you know your anger has moved beyond just a typical response and become a serious problem you need to do something about immediately, if not sooner!

Episodes of anger can vary in duration, frequency, and intensity, and you can experience them in the grocery store, in the car, at home, or just about anywhere your children act up. Even though we all experience a full range of sentiment, everything from mild frustration to severe forms of rage, there is no set way to measure your level of anger. Instead, to see how normal our anger is, we can count the frequency of its occurrence. According to MentalHelp.net, "on average an adult gets angry once a day, or annoyed three times a day," but that number has a lot to do with what happens within those 24 hours and how you handle and react to the things that occur. (They have obviously not hung out with my child after they ate too much sugar!)

Does this emotion have a purpose? Of course, it does. Anger, like most things, can be used constructively or destructively. At its core, anger is our warning sign, our mind's way of telling us something in our environment is not right. When you feel your heart rate rise, when adrenaline surges through you, and your muscles constrict, this is the body's natural response, readying you for action to rectify the situation, a simple motivator so you have the power to correct whatever irks you. How you express that anger will be the determining factor on whether you have a problem and are in turn causing issues for you, your family, and friends. For every action, there is an equal and opposite reaction, that is Newton's third law of energy, and it applies to anger as well because anger has energy, sometimes a lot, and other times just a little. Luckily, you control that power switch!

Anger Triggers & Causes

What brings on anger? (Some days it can be something as mundane as getting lukewarm coffee!) The answer to that question will, of course, vary from reader to reader. Think about that for more than a minute. What are the things that make you angry? When do you find yourself snapping? If you aren't immediately sure, make a note on your phone or keep a small journal with you to track these instances. Even if you already think you know, write down the time, the date, the location, the trigger, and the kind of reaction you have. This information will prove to be incredibly helpful and offer great insight later on. For now, let's return to that moment of ignition, there you are peeved and ready to blow, but these thoughts of animosity spring from what's happening in your life. When you understand what sets off your anger, you will be in a much better position to avoid or resolve the issues in the future, giving you and your family a far healthier and more balanced emotional life. In this section, we will share a few common anger triggers you should be looking out for.

Unfairness

How many times a day do you catch yourself thinking that was not fair? When someone does something unjust or is insensitive to you, it is very easy to feel everything from slightly irritated all the way to full on fury. Unfair treatment comes at you from all directions: your partner, your children, a total stranger, your boss, a coworker, a police officer, a customer service agent that is not being at all helpful. You may think your children watching TV while you make dinner alone is not fair; they may think you demanding they help make dinner after they've been in school all day and want to relax is not fair. As a trigger, unfairness stems from what we believe is fair. This varies greatly from person to person along with our definition of what is unjust. The main thing to remember is we live in an unfair world, so this trigger is everywhere! A calm and constructive reaction to unfairness will aid you in de-escalating those situations where it rears its ugly head.

Time Pressures

How hectic is your life? The world we live in is a very busy place. Everyone is multi-tasking and juggling, especially us parents. We have our work, our lives, our errands, alongside our children's school, clubs, sports, and friends. Balancing all of that sometimes seems impossible. When we don't have enough time for things, or we are running late, or we miss something, or we forget something entirely, it is very easy to have a meltdown. All of these demands on our time just increase our stress levels as we are pulled in so many different directions. Studies have shown that tempers have a shorter fuse when we are under pressure. I know I've screamed at my child to hurry up and get in the car when I'm running late. We all have.

When it comes to time pressures, the key to avoiding them is careful planning and following through on those plans. Make a schedule and post it in your kitchen: what needs to be done, when things need to be done, and who needs to do each task. Every member of the family can help in this arena. Have a family get together over pie or cake and make a life schedule. This will help you avoid that crazed rush when the minutes are running out. During my last visit with my sister, every morning I would hear her screaming at her kids that they had to leave for school NOW. There was never enough time in the morning. I suggested to her girls that they pick their clothes out the night before and pack their school bags, that way in the wee hours of the morning, when they were half awake, all they had to do was go to the desk, put on the outfit they had placed on the back of the chair, grab their backpack, and go downstairs, shortening the amount of time they needed and curtailing a round of shouting from their mother. That way, we spot the weakness (tired kids in the morning who can't get anything accomplished quickly), find a solution, and remove the issue. Now, my sister will have to find a new reason to yell at them.

Dishonesty

This trigger works in two ways. First, we have the habit of getting angry when someone lies to us. Your child tells you they did their homework, and they did not. They also did not break the lamp, or leave dirty dishes in the sink, or spill ink on your oriental rug. When people lie to us we feel betrayed, which instantly pisses us off and fills us with resentment.

The second way dishonesty triggers anger is when we lie to someone. In this case, we turn our anger inward against ourselves, but that does not mean we won't lash out at others. In fact, we generally do. When you are dishonest with your children, you will find yourself snapping at them more often. It took my mother a decade to tell us the real reason she and my father divorced, and, in the interim, any time I broached the subject I got yelled at - like it was my fault. We all do this in a misguided attempt to keep those we've lied to at a distance and to avoid coming to terms with our own dishonesty.

Disappointments

Life is filled with disappointments, and it is one of the most common anger triggers that we feel towards our children. As a parent, it is natural for you to want them to succeed, and when they don't it is normal to feel disappointed, but then you have to throw in a helping of self-blame for their failure and add in a side of fear that your child will suffer from the consequences of this poor performance. You want them to get good grades in school, but they don't. Disappointment + self-blame + fear for their failure = anger! Throughout our lives, disappointment will cause anger whenever you work hard to achieve something and then fail. If you are trying diligently to get promoted at work, but someone else gets the position, you are left feeling disappointed and angry. Whether you choose to direct that anger at someone else, be it your child, your partner, or the world, that part is up to you.

Personal Threats

What do we do when our safety or the safety of our

children is threatened? Peril awakens a very base, survivalist, self-preservation part of us we might not even know exists. I remember watching a father jump from a racing speed boat to go after his son who had fallen overboard. He did not hesitate or ask the driver to slow down, he simply jumped like a superhero. He broke his arm, but he saved his child. This was a case of physical danger, but a demonstration of instinctive preservation. We behave the same way when we are being personally attacked, either in the physical or the emotional sense. When someone criticizes you, or you criticize your child, the natural reaction will be one of self-preservation. If you are constantly telling your child they're doing things wrong, you can bet they will start to dislike you. Immediately, your reaction will be to resent the person and then try and stop these attacks. When anger is triggered by threats to self-esteem or identity, it usually results in a latent kind of lava-like fury that leaves you in a constant state of defensiveness and irritability. This, in turn, will make you even more likely to bubble up and boil over at the slightest of provocations, so watch out!

Discrimination and Prejudice

Discrimination as a cause of anger is similar to unfairness, but with more serious and far-reaching consequences. It might be unfair if your child did not get selected for the role in the school play because the teacher has another favorite student, but if they did not get that role due to the color of their skin or their ethnicity or their religious beliefs, that is a different story altogether. Discrimination and prejudice make the victim feel small and incapable and breeds underlying anger. Facing up to prejudice or discrimination will, of course, cause anger, as it should, but it instigates upset on both sides of the fence. Those on the receiving end of prejudice get angry, (and this would be a difficult situation in which to remain calm), while those doling out the prejudice do as well. Perpetrators of prejudice and discrimination are always yelling hateful slurs, especially when their victims try to stand up to them. Learning to handle discrimination calmly might be one of the hardest things you ever have to do.

Types of Anger

You might not realize this, but there are several different types of anger. Once you learn what they are, you should log the type in your notebook when you experience an emotional outburst. We can think of these types as various styles you might wear, and you can change your style daily, hourly, or never, like that guy who still sports a mullet. What style of anger do you find yourself wearing most often? Once you are aware of the different types, you can determine which one or ones are your go-to styles.

Passive Aggressive Anger

If you are the type to wear passive aggressive anger, it is more than likely you are a person who likes to avoid altercations. This style means you fill your pockets with all of your frustrating feelings and upset until they bulge at the seams. Often, you don't even realize you're angry because you keep shoving it down and away. These trapped, collected emotions often reveal themselves as something we know and love called sarcasm.

Assertive Anger

This style of anger is one of the most useful examples of a way you can use your frustration to manifest a positive change. Instead of avoiding confrontations or keeping anger trapped within, you choose to express these emotions in a strong, opinionated way that generates change in the world around you without being destructive or upset. Assertive anger is primarily seen as a powerful motivator that can help you achieve your desired dreams in life. This is a style you might want to try out for size!

Behavioral Anger

Do you physically lash out at the things or people that upset you? Have you smacked your child in frustration? Behavioral anger is often expressed with the hands. My mother loved to whack us with a wooden spoon or a hairbrush. Along with a verbal tirade, we had a physical outpouring of her anger. If you prefer this style, you probably feel overwhelmed by your emotions and then attack objects in a rage. This type of anger is generally unpredictable and can damage lives, mainly due to the negative effects it has on your relationships. If this is your style of anger, take a moment to calm down before doing something rash you may regret for the rest of your life. Walk away from the situation and use calming internal dialogue and breathing techniques until you regain control.

Chronic Anger

Just like the chronic pain you feel in your back, chronic anger is one that persists. Basically, you are angry all the damn time! This type looks like an overgeneralized resentment of broad categories of things - circumstance, people, or yourself. Chronic anger is the Scrooge of anger. If chronic anger is your style, you might suffer from a persistent state of irritation which can eventually lead to adverse effects on your health. Do you feel constantly annoyed at having to play the role of parent? Then chronic anger might be your style. To counteract it, figure out what triggers your anger. Write it down in your notebook. Once you have identified the cause, you will be better positioned to deal with these internal conflicts, find a way to outmaneuver them, and then forgive yourself for feeling them.

Critical or Judgmental Anger

When your child does not win in the Science Fair, do you get angry? If you get upset when a person fails you in some way, this is critical or judgmental anger. It is a righteous anger that is often directed at someone else's faults or rears its ugly head as a reaction to an injustice. This style of anger springs from a place of superiority that you somehow manage to justify. The best way to deal with it is to spend time looking at people, places, and things without judgement. In fact, use that as a mantra - no judgement!

Retaliatory Anger

A very common type of anger, this style appears as an instinctual response if you are bothered or provoked by someone. If your child yells at you, you will be quick to yell right back. This, my friends, is retaliatory anger, driven by the need to strike back at a supposed injury.

Self-Abusive Anger

Based on shame, this anger stems from feelings of low or no self-worth, humiliation, and hopelessness. This is when you really take out your anger on yourself! These adverse emotions get internalized and often reappear in your life as an unconstructive internal dialogue and/or self-harm. Alcohol, drug abuse, anorexia and bulimia are all signs of self-abusive anger. To cope with this style of anger, depending on the severity, you might want to consider seeking professional help or therapy or joining a support group. All of these options will provide you with different techniques to challenge and defeat the self-destructive thoughts you are experiencing. You may also find meditation helpful in dealing with these impulses.

Verbal Anger

As a parent, I think we are most familiar with verbal anger. We yell at our children to get them to do something or to stop doing something. The sad part is, this style of anger really hurts the person we turn it on, generally our little ones or our partners, and is considered psychological abuse. This style of anger comes out of us in the form of ridicule, sarcasm, shouting, threats, criticism, and blame. When it comes to this type of anger, take a deep breath, and think twice before uttering a word. The key to controlling this anger is delaying that urge to lash out. With practice, you will realize you can curb the bad habit of resorting to verbal abuse and instead replace it with a more positive assertive expression.

Volatile Anger

A volcano of anger types, you blow up at both little and small things, but once your volatile emotions are expressed you calm down. If this is you, then volatile anger is your anger style of choice. Unfortunately, just like a volcano, this type of anger can be very destructive to your relationships because people will fear triggering you and keeping you at bay. Remember my mother, and the 'don't poke the bear' rule in my house. Her destructive explosions were fearsome things to behold. To deal with this type of anger, find the triggers that precede these outbursts, and note them down so you can avoid them. You can also try using relaxation techniques like simple breathing to control your anger prior to explosion.

Impacts of Anger on You & Your Loved Ones

As we all know, anger is a natural emotion, built for a purpose. Not every outburst has to translate into something negative. It's our failure to manage our anger appropriately which can alienate family and friends. Aggressive behaviors can also increase your chances of early death and isolate you from social interactions, creating a clear negative link between this emotion and your health and lifespan. If you are upset all the time, your children will also be prone to bouts of anger and act defensively. You know the scene: everyone is angry and shouting, blood pressure increases, and stress levels rise. Further escalation can result in violence and then regret. When we compare anger to other emotions it is easy to see why it carries such negative attributes. After all, it sounds far better to be filled with happiness than anger, but it does have many positive attributes.

- Anger enables you to survive. This emotion drives you to be more vigilant and sharpen your focus. Without anger, you would be unable to quickly protect yourself against aggression.

- Anger provides a sense of control. This emotion can keep you from being and feeling like a victim. If you can express your anger appropriately, you'll be in a much better place than people who just constantly suppress their anger.

- Anger can motivate you to problem solve and be goal oriented. You can trigger anger when you face a person or obstacle which is keeping you from your needs, aspirations, or desires. Managed anger can ramp you up to overcome life's barriers. Use that energy anger provides to attain important goals!

- Injustice makes us angry! Probably the preeminent use of anger is to help overcome injustice and pressure society to bring about positive change.

- Anger supports hopefulness and protects your values. Anger pushes you to focus on what you hope to achieve. Often when you get angry, you are then filled with a positive sensation and heightened sense of enthusiasm regarding your ability to change an outcome. Let this feeling drive you toward a desired goal or further stand up for your beliefs!

- Anger can provide you with inner strength. When someone tries to stop you from achieving, anger can be your guardian angel, giving you the power to persevere. Let this emotion help you remove obstacles in your path and reach those goals (as long as you curb your anger at the point it becomes harmful)!

- Anger can be used to help you obtain an advantage. When something you think is important is belittled, your anger will definitely assert itself, but this can improve the situation. Let your anger cause others to rethink their position and change a stubborn mind or two!

- Anger can lead to increased communication and cooperation. Your anger will let your loved ones know they may need to pay better attention to your words. Let your anger help you stand up for yourself and challenge other points of view to find better solutions!

- Anger can push you positively and make you a better person and a better parent. It can help you figure out who you really are. Let anger push you to search for deeper issues that would normally remain hidden! Look in your notebook. Don't you know yourself better now?

Too often as a parent we tend to think of anger only

in negative terms, so now that we know how many positive things this emotion can do, let's use it to encourage our optimism, insight, and self-improvement.

Parental Anger: Cause & Effects

Now that we know the things anger can do to help us become better people and parents, we must flip to the other side of the emotional coin and look at the negative aspects of the sentiment. Almost any emotion in the extreme can be destructive, and this goes double for anger. We might feel completely vindicated for expressing it, but there are far too many times our anger is not proportional to the occurrence or at all justified. What causes you to blow up will vary from person to person and from day to day. You should put the source of your bursts of anger in your notebook to see if there is a pattern or repetition. For every cause, there is an effect, and becoming aware of the effects of anger, both on ourselves and on our family, is crucial to good parenting. Below, I have identified three areas where anger can cause destruction in your life when taken to the extreme.

Feeling

As we all know, if we let it, anger can be an overpowering emotion, which is why we need to use our intellect to control it, instead of letting it control us. Think about how you are feeling, what is the best way to show your emotions, and how you can do that without going to your angry place. The amygdala, or the seat of emotions in the brain, must coordinate responses with the higher cortical centers for thinking, planning, and analyzing.

But when our feelings are cut off from the thinking centers of the brain, that's when anger takes control. Having this emotion in the driver's seat usually means we are headed for a crash landing! You know those moments when you can't think clearly because you are consumed by anger. How many crimes of passion or revenge take place because the person is controlled by rage and in that moment has no problem killing someone? Only when the anger dissipates do they realize what they did was wrong, and then they hire a very good lawyer! That disconnect between thinking and feeling suddenly makes anger a very dangerous emotion. We make poor decisions when we fail to think things through and stupidly act on those destructive feelings.

How many times have you thought you just feel anger too quickly? You jump right into that emotion with both feet, and a little error or inconvenience can make you explode. It does depend on your threshold for anger. If you are the type of person who is easily irritated by the slightest provocation, this could be problematic for you and your family, especially if your reaction is always an overreaction.

If you get upset when your child dumps out all the

shampoo on the bathroom floor simply because they like to hear the squirt noise (true story), okay, but if you blow up at them for leaving the top off the bottle and a little water gets inside, then you might want to take a good, hard look in the mirror. When even the littlest things trigger big displays of anger, that is when we are in trouble.

The worst, or best, part is we have a sense of catharsis when we act on this anger. We feel a purging, a cleansing, a liberation when we let ourselves explode like that. Catharsis is the release of emotions, that relief we get after spewing those negative feelings all over whoever was unlucky enough to be standing in our path. You know you feel good after you've shouted and confronted someone who's offended you! Just like there is a sense of satisfaction if you punch someone who has hurt you physically. We do it as children, strike out physically or verbally. This makes acting out of anger addicting! You can actually get a high from exerting your dominance on another person.

But feelings are usually temporary. They come and go. They change. However, if you experience anger for extended periods of time, you can actually get physically sick. Anger releases your stress hormones - adrenaline and norepinephrine. This pushes the body into fight or flight mode, making your heart pump faster, making you sweat, constricting your blood vessels, affording you the energy to confront or avoid danger. When that danger is no longer there, the body should shift into a relaxation mode, but if you are perpetually angry even when the stressor is gone, your hormones maintain this attack mode. That means you're signing up for hypertension, strokes, heart attacks, or cancer. In the long run, your body will deteriorate faster the longer you are angry, so, be like Elsa, and let it go!

Thinking

Did you know anger reduces your ability to think clearly? When we don't control our emotions, anger overpowers our thinking process and the result is bad decisions. If we're angry, we think danger is all around us, ready to strike at a moment's notice. We can't think clearly about anything, and that's when, inevitably, we do something impulsively idiotic.

If somebody punches you, most people want to return the favor. You won't stop to wonder if they hit you accidentally or tell yourself fighting in public is inappropriate. Your instinct is to simply slug them right back. We get tunnel vision and fail to see details that might be important to the situation. Our focus is on the danger, so we react impulsively. Nine times out of ten, these are poor decisions we regret in the future.

When we are constantly angry, we also tend to focus on the nature of people and not the act that was committed.

This is called "correspondence bias." We judge people by that one bad thing they did instead of the big picture. Turning an evil act into an evil person, is something we as parents love to do. If a child in our kid's class pushes someone on the playground, we tell them not to hang around that person and label them as bad. For some reason, we tend to see people as good or bad, with no in-betweens. Sometimes, based on just one event.

Did you know anger makes us think that bad things are going to happen? When you are in a bad mood, you are in combat mode (minus the camouflage), so the way you look at the world will be through anything but rose-colored glasses. The phone rings. It is your child's school calling. Instantly, you think your kid blew up the science lab when they are actually being inducted into the Honor Society. Anger makes us generalize things for the worse.

Our memory also plays a big part in our emotions. If we think about our child's birthday party, Halloween night when the kids decided to watch horror movies, or a grandfather's funeral, we associate a feeling with each of these events. We believe birthday celebrations are happy occasions, a horror movie is terrifying, and funerals are sad. When we experience similar scenarios, we tend to attach our previous emotions to them. This is also very true of anger. If one child always forgets to clean out the litter box leaving you constantly standing over that box shouting at them to come clean it, every time you see cat poop you will automatically get angry and blame that child, even when it might (and usually is) the other one's turn to clean the litter box. Memory brings back the negative emotions attached to the scene alongside our tendency to never forget. That's why they say, you can forgive but not forget!

The Effects on Parent's Actions

Are you the type of person who acts impulsively on their feelings? If you are, that means you are primed for destructive bouts of anger. If you catch your child eating in their room when you told them not to bring food upstairs, there are lots of ways you can react. You could simply take the food away. You could stop buying their favorite snacks for a month. You could make them clean their room and their sibling's room and take out all the recycling and compost to make up for this infraction of house rules. You could also stand there and scream at them until you are red in the face and they are crying, or even worse smack them. Find ways to resolve a problem without making a bad situation worse!

They say timing is everything, and it even plays a role in anger. When we get upset, we want to take immediate action! The period between the offense and our act of vengeance is usually short, but this cuts out the time we should take for thinking things over. For some reason, when we can't right the wrong immediately, we get even more hurt and anxious as if by delaying retribution we are experiencing more injustice. Which, of course, makes no sense, because if you know who egged your house on Halloween, egging their house right back or next week won't change the circumstance (your house got egged), but your gut reaction is to go out straight away for payback. The longer you wait, the more steamed you get!

Sometimes, the anger you feel and your reaction will not be appropriate to the offense. If your child breaks your favorite vase while playing ball in the house and you smack his bum with your belt and make him go hungry for a day, this would be a case where the punishment might not fit the crime. You say the vase is important to you, it might be very valuable, hence your overreaction, and you feel that retaliation was warranted because of the pain. Punishing your child for what they did, for that pain they caused you, is important to you, but that can also make you exaggerate your actions and go too far.

Blaming is another common effect of anger. When we get angry, our focus is directed out at another person, not on ourselves. We tend to blame other people for whatever bad thing happened, and dismiss our own culpability in the incident. The mantra of an angry person is, "I am always right and you are always wrong." This can lead to some embarrassing situations for you. The next door neighbor's kid slashes your son's bicycle tires, and you storm out to harass the kid and their parents. Then, you find out your child started the fight two days ago when he pushed the boy's head in a school toilet and gave him a bloody nose. How quick we are to blame others before we think or learn about the entire situation!

But anger, like all emotions, must be expressed. I remember learning primal scream therapy as a teenager. How great that felt to just stand in the woods or at the top of the hill and scream as loud as I possibly could. Try it in your car with the music blaring. Grab the wheel with all of your might and scream, long and loud, until you just fizzle out. Picture your anger leaving your body along with your scream. Trust me, it helps! When we suppress our anger, we can become depressed and even suffer from IBS, irritable bowel syndrome. Nobody wants that! We already mentioned how not being able to express your anger can cause eating disorders. Carrying anger around with us can convert the emotion into physical symptoms like headaches, vomiting, or diarrhea. In some cases of chronic anger, there are instances when normally calm and collected people suddenly launch into a violent rage. This pent-up anger can be destructive to you and your family. Better out, than in, so find healthy ways to release it!

Anger is a vicious cycle and not one you want to perpetuate. The anger you release on your family gets absorbed by them. In time, they will release that anger on other people. More than likely, that anger will also be directed back at you. My sister always gets so upset when her children yell at her, but she yells at them, about everything, much like my mother. When I pointed out the cycle and reminded her how much we hated when our mother yelled at us, she acknowledged the hurt she felt, she admitted the pain she feels currently when her children yell at her. Yet she has done nothing to change her actions. Instead of yelling at them to put their dishes in the sink, she could just tell them. My daughter has only raised her voice to me occasionally, but as soon as she does I tell her not to speak to me in that tone, and she stops. You have to nip those actions in the bud or they perpetuate! Mahatma Gandhi had it right when he said, "An eye for an eye makes the whole world blind."

Early signs of anger include:

- quickening of the pulse
- stirring of the stomach
- feeling tense
- quickening of the breath

- a flushed face

- straining of the shoulders

- gripping your hands or grinding your jaw

- perspiring

Negative Thinking

Another effect of anger is negative thinking. This is extremely normal when you're upset. Yet it further aggravates the situation. Some typical negative parental thoughts are the following: "Nobody in this house helps me with anything, I need to do everything myself so things are right, or whenever I clean something it just gets messy again two seconds later." We are exacerbating the situation with our mindset, and we need to retrain our brains and reshape not only how we think, but also how we parent.

When we stop to think about it, there's generally a reason for a child's terrible conduct. Sure, it could be an issue at school like a bully tormenting them or maybe their parents are going through a divorce, but other times the reason is that the child's parents can't handle their own anger and this young one learned from them how to be nasty. It is up to us as parents to make sure this does not happen! If your family's relationship as a team isn't solid, then start to find things that bring you together peacefully and happily. Get rid of the negative thoughts, shut out the world for a moment and focus on working through any issues you might have in a positive way. Talk it out, whatever it is, but discuss it calmly and tranquilly. This makes all the difference!

Have a weekly meeting to chat through any issues or upsets. There are so many ways to avoid going to that angry place to solve problems, because screaming generally creates more issues than it ever fixes. Most importantly, if they see you are quick to anger, and they believe that's an entirely normal reaction, expect them to respond that way in short order. When life gets them down or lets them down, they will also be the ones screaming their heads off. If they see you detonate at the slightest thing, then congratulations soon enough you will probably have an angry child on your hands.

Anger and Discipline

Angry discipline is not proper discipline because, simply put, you, yourself, are not being disciplined. So, how do you discipline your child? How do you ensure they conduct themselves properly, are polite, and make the right decisions? Controlling your anger is about restraint - and if your rage comes out while you are attempting to correct your children's behavior, that is not positive discipline.

It should be no surprise that your anger influences how you parent. It influences how you converse with and raise your children, but you need to agree about family issues and present a unified front, especially if you have a partner. The whole good cop, bad cop scenario might work for you, or it might not. These are things that trial and error will determine while you find what works for your family. How do your children respond? Do they change their bad habits? They need to know where your limits are and if one parent says yes, and the other no, those sneaky devils might set you up to contend with each other.

Angry discipline also involves picking fights with your children over the smallest of things. Having unreasonable standards that they can never hope to meet and then yelling at them about it is another sad side effect, so make sure your guidelines are age appropriate and reasonable. I remember being yelled at for coloring outside the lines, still on the paper, but outside the given lines. At any age, this is unreasonable because it really does not matter! Pick your battles, and make sure they are only the important ones.

Your Anger and Your Child

Children just see you as an angry parent, and that makes you harder to love. Try and look at it from your child's perspective, that is a big part of how I fixed my problems. If you are constantly yelling at your kid, they will also start to think you don't love them. Their self-confidence and self-worth will start to crumble. I know mine did, and still does a bit. It is something I have to continually work on. If we as parents don't show them they are loved and cherished, they will go out into the world thinking nobody can love or cherish them because mommy or daddy couldn't. Your anger will have some long reaching consequences that can deter your children from thinking they are worth loving. This can lead them to wind up in abusive or negative relationships in the future. What goes around, comes around they say, so, in that same line, if you strike your child, they, in turn, will be much more likely to smack others.

Breaking the Endless Loop

I know what it is like to live with a parent who is constantly angry. It's not fun. I can't think of any happy moments we shared when I was a child, and that's sad. I decided I wanted my little one to have so many fond memories she found it hard to choose her favorite, and she does! We can break the cycle of anger, but first we have to acknowledge it is there. Next, we have to see where it comes from and why. Then we have to stop, breathe, calm down, and pause before we react. Life (and children) will always give us reasons to get angry, but the key is to stop that anger from preventing you from reacting to your child in a positive and valuable way when they do something wrong.

Face up to Your Anger

Take a good, hard look at the way in which you express your anger and disappointment. Do you hold it inside until you detonate? Do you let it eek out in biting, overcritical comments that pick apart your child's character? Do you scream it out, overwhelming others with your rage? Just remember, your child learns by example, and they will certainly emulate the way you express your anger, so make sure it is something you want them to replicate.

Understand Why You're Angry

Once you have determined and kept track of the causes of your outbursts in your notebook, this is when you have to take those extra moments to really look at the scenario which made you angry. If you dress your child to go to a party, and while you're finishing getting ready they go and play in the mud, ruining their good clothes, you might think you have the right to be upset. But let's stop and examine this scenario for a moment. They did not understand that getting messy would cause issues. They just felt like playing because they were bored and wanted to pass the time. Screaming at the child does not accomplish anything aside from upsetting both of you. Take a moment to breathe and really look at a situation before and even after you get angry to better determine why you went there and if you were justified to do so. No one said this was going to be easy! Seeing your child coated in mud right when you have to leave is fuel for that internal fire, but this is when managing your anger comes into play. Something we will show you how to do, or at least improve on, in the next chapter.

Chapter Summary

- We learned what anger is and its purpose in your life.
- We learned the different types of anger and how they affect you and your children.
- We learned to recognize anger's many causes or triggers.
  .

Chapter Two
Managing Parental Anger

"Now, I know I got to take. Control, now I've got a lot. Control to get what I want. Control, never gonna stop. Control, now I'm all grown up." – Janet Jackson

Let's just accept the fact right now that as parents we are going to get angry. There is no way you will not encounter things that irk you, things that piss you off, things that annoy you (deeply), and things that make you want to scream out loud in the middle of the supermarket. That is part and parcel to having a child. Thinking otherwise is just setting yourself up for supreme failure. I advise keeping a calendar, and marking each day with a heart if you do not get angry within that 24 hours in relation to your role as someone's mother or father. After a month, look and see where you are on the angry parent scale. Use this point as your baseline, and let's look to raise next month's number of hearts. We get upset for so many reasons, but at the crux of it is our kids aren't doing what they're told or conforming to our expectations.

You might want to peruse a parenting book to find out what are normal things to expect from your children during each stage of development and growth. They can be helpful because a lot of us expect far too much from our children at certain ages. What we do when we get angry is up to us to control because the spectrum of upset can swing from that mildly annoyed tone we take when they won't stop talking to us when we are on the phone all the way to an eruption of rage and fury or even a physical attack. We get enraged to shield ourselves from a threat, but what we need to remember is, although they may at times threaten our sanity, these little misbehaving people are not actual threats, and we are the ones enhancing the level of drama by getting angry. Channel your inner Janet Jackson and find your control to get what you want! Put the song on repeat, if need be, or make it your mantra, because losing control will have repercussions on you and could have serious effects on your child's growth.

Now that you have accepted the fact that getting angry is completely normal, let's turn our focus on how we should react when we feel overwhelmed by this emotion. The most important thing is to try and stay calm and not take our anger out on our children. The problem is, they're our kids, so they will know exactly how to push our buttons! If we lose our ability to think clearly and simply act out, either verbally or physically, we are regressing and behaving no better than our children. The best thing to do is not act or discipline a child while you are upset. Stop, breathe, and take a step back from the situation, mentally or physically, or both. Walk out of the room, hum your new mantra song, but take a second before you do something rash that you will most likely regret later. What sort of role model will you make if you scream at your little one? This will tell them that yelling and screaming is how adults solve their problems.

Here are a few steps to take when you find yourself about to blow a fuse:

1. Calm down before you speak or discipline your little ones.

2. Put yourself in a timeout! If it works for the kids, it can work for you too!

3. Don't act on your anger, but do listen to it.

4. Put limits on things before you get upset—time limits, volume limits, etc.

5. Talk calmly with them about the hurt or disappointment that is causing your anger instead of just

expressing it by yelling or screaming.

6. Choose your words carefully and pay attention to your tone of voice.

7. Examine any fear or hurt causing your anger and let it go.

8. Here's a tough one—accept the fact that you might be part of the problem.

9. Find effective ways you can discipline your kids that reward and encourage good behavior.

10. Pick your battles wisely! The more happy interactions you have with your little ones, the more likely they are to listen to you.

11. As a family, decide what are the acceptable ways to express anger and post the different options on your refrigerator so everybody knows.

12. Do not make threats about disciplinary issues unless you plan to follow through on them.

13. No matter what, avoid the use of physical punishments!

The best way to see how your anger affects your children is to put yourself in their shoes. Picture someone twice or three times your size coming at you, looming over you and screaming, shaking their fist, yelling, or doing whatever it is you do when you are mad. Now, remember that this screaming giant is the person you love most in the world, the one who feeds you and bathes you, the person you depend on the most, the one who gives you everything, including your self-esteem. Look at that picture, take those feelings, multiply them tenfold, and you might understand what your child experiences when you lose your cool.

Screaming at your child is already scary enough, but what if you go further? What happens when you spank them or hit them? When we yell, it affects their self-esteem, but when we hit this can lead to ongoing issues like lower IQs and later on things like substance abuse and the inability to have healthy relationships. Make a commitment to yourself not to yell, curse, or hit your child. Remember, if you are screaming at them, that's a tantrum. Who is the child here?

Obviously, we are bound to get angry at some point, at many points, but unless we want our emotions to do lasting damage to our kids it is up to us to take responsibility for what these ill expressed feelings can do to our little ones. When we are angry parents the following issues can arise in our children:

—They have very low levels of sympathy and pity for others.

—They are certainly more disobedient and aggressive.

—They are more likely to become delinquents.

—They struggle with adjusting to the things life throws at them.

—They can experience issues far into their adult lives including social alienation, depression, spousal abuse, and lower levels of financial or career success.

Looking at that list, we definitely don't want any of those things for our kids, so in order to be better parents we need to learn more about where our anger comes from and then find ways we can respond to that emotion in a healthy manner, one that is not detrimental to us or our little ones. When you manage to do that, there are several positive things that can happen in your life. You are much less likely to cause any emotional or physical damage when you are angry. You will be much calmer when you deal with your kids. You can handle your anger, when it comes, in a healthy way. You will feel more confident and in control of yourself and your life. You won't fear your anger or the anger of your child. You won't feel the need to get angry because you have learned better responses, and if you or your children do get upset, you will be able to cope with it. The abatement and control of your anger will give you a much more stress-free home, one where your kids will feel happier, healthier, safer, and filled with a higher sense of self-esteem. Doesn't that sound wonderful? Now, let's get to work making that happen for you!

During my last visit with my family, I noticed my sister constantly yelling at her children for one thing or another, for big things and for little things. It was a constant yell fest! One girl left her milk on the table overnight, the other had been drawing on her arms and hands with a pen, one left a bookbag on the kitchen floor, the other was upstairs when my sister wanted her downstairs, nobody ever put their phones in the chargers when they came home from school. Everyday instructions for life were not communicated in a normal, calm tone, they were always yelled like a stream of military commands, and my sister was the mean drill sergeant everyone despised. Ironically, my sister got very upset, to the point that she cried to me, because her kids started yelling back at her. Imagine my non surprise at this! Yet somehow, she was shocked to see the behavior she kept showing her children coming back at her, and the worst part was she was hurt by it.

I told her to imagine what it is like to be yelled at all day, every day just to get simple things accomplished in the house. I told her to remember what it was like when we were kids because that is exactly what our mother did. She was perpetuating this cycle of anger, and now her twelve-year-old twins were dishing it right back to her. The fact that it made her cry was what really drove home my feelings on the issue. If being yelled at is making you sad and making you cry, don't you think it is doing the exact same thing to your little ones? Of course, it is! She is teaching them that instead of talking about something or asking nicely, they need to scream at one another to communicate, and, boy, do they ever! They are learning this behavior directly from her, and nobody is happy about it. Now, everyone in the house is carrying around this anger and resentment towards one another. In the next chapter, we will further discuss the causes and signs of children's anger and show you how you can help your kids deal with these pent up emotions.

Chapter Summary

- Managing parental anger is an ongoing learning process
- There are many things you can do to control your anger and improve your response when you do get upset with your children.
- Your anger will have long and short term negative effects on your children.

Chapter Three
Child Psychology

Did you know that understanding the normal and abnormal psychological patterns of your child can help you to better communicate and connect with them? It's time to take a look inside your child's mind to see what makes them tick and what ticks them off. Now that you have learned how to better deal with your anger, you can teach your little ones coping mechanisms for managing their strong emotions, and help them progress and thrive in each new stage of their development. In this chapter, we will look at the causes and signs of children's anger at different ages, show you what is considered normal and identify when there might be a problem, as well as offer solutions on what you can do to help them deal with the upsets of life which are bound to come their way, no matter how much we wish to protect them.

Causes of Children's Anger

What makes your kids mad? How often are they getting upset? Sometimes it's not getting what they want when they want it, or being told to clean their room, or being bullied at school, or arguing with a sibling. There are so many things that can make our little ones angry, but it is our job as parents to observe our children and see what makes them unhappy and why, to notice if they are constantly angry or bothered or anxious and to find a way to fix that for them. That's what good parents do.

Very often their anger is a mask for another emotion they might be feeling such as:

Worry or anxiety— they are being bullied, they are afraid any basic need in their lives might not be met, they are anxious about their school performance, social pressures, or meeting your expectations, etc.

Embarrassment or shame– they hate their skin (acne) or their looks, or their bodies, they carry feelings of worthlessness and stupidity around with them, they feel awkward in front of other kids, perhaps a sibling is much smarter than they are, etc.

Sadness or loneliness— you are yelling at them, you

work long hours and they never see you, they have no one to play with them, they aren't good at making friends, their parents are arguing, you are going through a divorce, a death in the family, etc.

Disappointment— they did not make the team or get the grades they wanted, they did not get invited to go somewhere, they did not win an election at school, you broke a promise to them, etc.

Jealousy— of other kids for having expensive things, of their siblings, of getting your time and attention, of a boyfriend or girlfriend, etc.

Hurt— they've been rejected by you, a friend, a sibling, they've suffered a break up of a friend or romantic nature, a friend or family member betrayed them, etc.

Frustration— at their lack of friends, at their bad grades, at a physical impediment, at their inability to control their lives, etc.

Guilt— they hurt someone or broke something, they let you down, watch out because they can feel responsible for your divorce, they are being abused, etc.

Fear— of something like spiders or someone like a teacher or a step parent, of a personal shortcoming or illness, of being a victim of abuse, of not having enough to eat, etc.

Any one of these underlying emotions can cause your little one to get angry, and these feelings are common in all of us, children and adults alike. Try to identify which of these things might be coming before the outburst. That anger occurs due to one of these or a mix of these everyday emotions. If we can change what comes before and after the anger, we can then stop the anger from frothing out in the first place. This is what the premise of behavior modification therapy is based on. In most of these cases, your child's anger has nothing to do with you, so don't take it personally. Your kids are merely using that emotion as a shield to hide what is really bothering them, but it is your job to play detective and find out what the real cause is.

There are a few very serious conditions that can cause severe tantrums in children, things like learning disorders, autism, anxiety issues, and Attention Deficit/Hyperactivity Disorder or ADHD, Oppositional Defiant Disorder or ODD, Asperger's, or depression. If your little one is having a meltdown in school because they do not feel like doing something a teacher asks, it might be more than just a bad day. If this behavior continues or worsens, it could be time to take them to a doctor. Don't fret, there are many things a child like this can learn in order to deal with these emotions in a constructive and healthy way and stop flying off the handle.

How does your child show they are angry? Most kids have their go to responses. Do they yell at you? Do they throw things around their room? Do they get into fights at school or with their siblings? Do they have an insane fit of rage? Do they get frustrated if they can't solve a problem or don't win a game and throw all the cards on the floor or tip the board game over? Do they blame you for all of their problems? This is like being a good poker player, because you need to learn your children's tells, pull them aside and talk to them about whatever is bothering them.

Things that upset your children will also change as they grow up, so let's take a look at a quick breakdown of issues you are likely to run into through the years.

Age 0-2: What makes your child angry at this stage might be things you can't relate to, but you should be aware that hunger is expressed by crying out—and they get hungry a lot! That little bundle of joy can only get your attention one way, by crying. So, be prepared for gas, poop, too hot, too cold, hungry, thirsty, bored, and uncomfortable to be communicated through that same scream. Your baby is not angry. It is just one of those other wants or needs or issues rearing up and needing you to resolve it.

When that little being starts to get mobile, other issues will quickly arise. Now, they will get mad if you try to impede their progress in moving, walking, and feeding themselves. They don't want you to stop them! They are trying to be just like you. You can avert some meltdowns by offering them safe ways to keep on trying that new crawl or shuffle, get rid of clothing that constricts their motion, and attend to their cries of frustration or discomfort rapidly so they feel loved and cared for throughout this stage of development.

Age 3-4:Ahh, preschool! A time for them to interact with their peers and develop a whole new array of annoying behaviors. Where cries of, "she took my crayon!" and "that's mine" will be the norm. These little ones have short attention spans and high levels of frustration when things don't go their way, which generally emerges as anger. Keep them busy, but be flexible. These are willful creatures who won't always want to do what you want, when you want it, so inform them of your plans to remove any shock that they can't play with the clay all afternoon because you have to go to the market. Make sure they have their own space to play in, somewhere they feel comfortable to just be them and probably make a mess. Preplanning for a mess is a good way to avert disasters and episodes of anger.

Age 5-6: What a fun time you'll have when your child starts showing their anger physically first and then verbally. They might be better able to communicate with you, but they do not have the control we would like them to have just yet. At this age, they will come to know the terms "right and wrong" and how they should and should not act, but this does not mean they will always do what you want them to do. Lots of things won't be fair to them and even more things will hurt their feelings, so be prepared for those hands on the hips moments and lots of talks about feelings. Talking to your child about how they feel is one of the healthiest things you can do, and it is also one of the most helpful. You will see this idea stated and restated throughout the book in a myriad of ways. Hug them and calmly talk to them!

Helping Your Little Ones Deal with Anger

Now that you know how their anger might manifest and for what reasons, let's discuss how we can help them deal with these emotions. It is up to you to show them how to best express the feelings of frustration and upset they are bound to encounter in everyday life. If you or your child spills a glass of juice on the table, don't yell! Calmly and kindly show them how to fix the problem. Let them spray the cleaner or wipe the rag so they feel like they have also been part of the solution. You can show them better ways to express their anger! If they are mad, you can try primal scream therapy with them, yelling together to let out the bad feelings. You could also whack a tennis ball or kick a soccer ball and tell them to envision the ball as whatever is bothering them. Sprint out that anger and do quick runs with them, if you add in a yell while you run you will really be able to let out some of that pent up emotion. It is up to you to teach these little ones how to vocalize and share what is bothering them with you.

Make sure you keep an open line of communication, and if a one on one is too daunting, bring in the puppets and act it out. Let them talk about what they are feeling: mad, frustrated, sad, depressed, anxious, lonely. Have the puppets talk about their emotions or just sit and talk to your child about what they are feeling. Put some play dough on a table and let them smash out their anger into the colorful putty. Most importantly, you need to be ready for issues to crop up, and have solutions in your pockets, handbag, or backpack. If you have not already realized, kids are always hungry! I never left home without snacks and water in my bag. It is a very simple thing, but do you know how many cranky moments can be avoided this way—far too many to count! If you have a snack and a water bottle in your bag, you won't have a whining hungry or thirsty child in your car.

Here are a few other ways we can help our children deal with the things that upset them.

Develop anger management skills like deep breathing, primal scream therapy, or have them keep an anger journal. Make an anger scale so they can explain if they are a one (a little bit upset) or a ten (a volcano ready to explode), and try to make it fun to talk about your feelings. Being upset is nothing to hide, and chatting about it with them is the healthiest thing you can ever do.

Never let their tantrums run your life. Sure, it might be a heck of a lot easier to give in to your child's cries for more cake or more time on the swing or whatever thing they currently find so important in their life that they are willing to scream their heads off for it. Giving in to terrorist demands is never a good idea, because you are training them that this is how they get what they want. Trust me when I say, those bad behaviors will play out on repeat in your life for years to come. If they scream at you for that cookie, and it's almost dinner time and they should not have it, do not give it to them. Tell them to stop screaming. Explain that this is not the way to talk to anybody. Walk out of the room if you have to. Ignore them until they calm down and then explain the right way to ask for things or express they are upset. But nip it in the bud the first time! Talk them down off of that ledge, make sure they understand that you are there, and you are listening, but calmly let them know there is a better way to communicate their needs, wants, and desires and it is not by screaming at the top of their lungs.

Create a way to calm down. Find a fun way in which you and your child can come out of a tantrum together or separately. I was told to sit on the stairs and think about what I had done. Now, if we make it a little less harsh, add in a comfortable corner of their room or a cozy chair, or a teepee they go to when they (or you) need to find peace of mind, it can become the calm down spot. You can tell them to go there when they are feeling upset to take a moment, breathe, and collect themselves. Tell them that chair or tepee or corner had magical calming properties. This makes it fun. "You might even create a calm-down kit. This could include your child's favorite coloring books and some crayons, a fun book to read, stickers, a favorite toy, or lotion that smells good" (Morin, Very Well Family, 2021). When they start to get upset, tell them to go grab it so they can help themselves feel happier. This shows your child that they are not only responsible for their emotions, but they can also control them.

Be consistent with your discipline! Be aware that saying they can't watch TV as a punishment and then not following through will completely undermine your authority. That is just setting yourself up for disaster. Always follow through on any consequence or punishment you tell them they will have for a naughty behavior. When your little one disobeys, make sure they are consistently punished every time. If they happen to break a vase or a plate or a game, have them fix it or do chores around the house to pay to replace it. They need to see that there are repercussions to bad behavior.

Avoid violent video games, television shows, and movies. Instead, find happy things for your child to watch or play that encourage learning or entertainment on a playful level. Puzzles and puzzle games are great. Things that demonstrate positive and nonviolent resolutions to problems. We played Pac Man, and although we ate ghosts we did not kill anybody. There are lots of modern or vintage games without violence, death, and destruction. Board games and card games can entertain without issues. If your child is already anger prone, the last thing you need is for them to be playing first-person-shooter or battle royal games that heighten and glorify that type of emotion and resolution to situations.

Child Psychology

"Child psychology is the study of subconscious and conscious childhood development. Child psychologists observe how a child interacts with their parents, themselves, and the world, to understand their mental development." [5] We all want our children to be healthy and happy, but figuring out when their actions and behaviors cross that line into officially unhealthy can often be difficult for us as parents to determine. We don't have that step back advantage, and we are not officially trained in these things.

Plus, it is hard to admit that we can't solve the problem ourselves. It is even harder to come to terms with the fact that your child might need professional help. If you aren't sure, if you are even questioning, then it might be time to turn to a child psychologist for assistance. They can easily determine what is normal and abnormal and guide you in how to better relate and handle your child if you cannot manage helping them cope with their issues by yourself. They can also detect things that might be detrimental to your child that you might not be able to, such as learning issues, anxiety, childhood traumas, and behavioral issues like hyperactivity. They will look at the physical, emotional or social, and mental development of your child to determine exactly what is going on, and what the heck is going wrong, and then offer you solutions on how to deal with these problems. If things are not that dire, and you are ready and willing to take the time to invest in your little one, then there are many readily available solutions that you can try without bringing in professional help.

First and foremost, understanding your child's anger, the signs they show when they get upset, and how you can help them express these emotions in a healthy way is something you can definitely do, but it will require effort and planning and time, so be prepared to invest in all three of those things. You need to commit to making these changes in your life, if you have not already done so. If your child has angry outbursts that are scary or go beyond what is considered normal or expected in a given situation, and especially if your little one's anger interferes with their relationships and quality of life, it is time for you to take immediate action. I cannot stress how important it is to teach your little ones the skills they need to deal with their feelings in a healthy way. Nobody wants to play with the ranting child on the playground or the kid that won't share or the bully that pushes others.

Your children are going to get angry, they are going to yell and they are going to cry. Knowing that these situations will arise does give you the upper hand. You can be prepared for them! However, how you handle those impending emotional explosions is what will make or break your child, and why it is so important to deal with these situations calmly, consistently, and intelligently. If you are the one screaming at your kid to pick up their room, who is in control? Not you! Dealing with them rationally, in a way that will help them evolve into lovely human beings, requires us to have emotional intelligence or EQ, and that is what we will discuss in the next chapter. If you don't know what that is, then we will explain it and show you just how you can raise your EQ.

Chapter Summary

- We discussed what things might be causing our children to get angry.
- We then showed ways you can help your child deal with that anger.
- We talked about what child psychology is and how a child psychologist might be able to help you in certain situations you aren't equipped to deal with alone.

Chapter Four
Emotional Intelligence in Parenting

Emotional intelligence is basically your ability to handle your own emotions, to understand them and to manage them, in a stress-free way. Wouldn't that be nice? In parenting, emotional intelligence is more like two things instead of one. First, you have to connect with your own emotions and express them to your child in a healthy way, and second, you have to be aware of and accurately identify your child's emotions, those they express and those they don't, and help them feel safe and loved enough to be able to express their feelings to you. You might think that it sounds like a lot of work, but it is worth it. If you are emotionally intelligent, it stands to reason your child will also be emotionally intelligent, and this is definitely a win-

win. So, now that you know you have an EQ as well as an IQ, here is how it can help both you and your child.

Characteristics of EQ

Emotional intelligence, otherwise known as your EQ, will help you clean up the emotional messes life makes when we are going about your day to day. That's how I like to look at it, so let's clean up our own MESSS with some heightened emotional intelligence!

Motivation— Why do you want to be a good parent? Look at why you decided to take on this role in the first place. How motivated are you to succeed at this job? No matter what problems you face as a parent, try and remain positive and optimistic, even when you have a breakdown or a misstep. Always look for one good thing that came from even the worst of situations. Did you apologize after you lost your temper with your child? Okay, that's a good thing!

Empathy— Having empathy as a parent is imperative to your success. Put yourself in the shoes of your children, and try to see things from their perspective. Pay close attention to your child's body language and develop the ability to read their emotions without them having to tell you. Most importantly, respond to the way your children feel. Do not ignore their emotions or bury them or hope they will go away. They won't. Give your feelings and their feelings a voice or a stage on which they can be heard without fear of judgement or repercussion— just discussion! Dinner time is always a great place to open up the table to discuss things. Make it part of your daily routine.

Self-awareness— To thine own self be true, they say, and knowing your strengths and weaknesses, confronting them, and admitting them to yourself and your children can be a revelation. Sit down with a journal, and record (at that dinner time daily discussion) what everyone in the family has as their strengths and weaknesses so you can work on them together. If you get upset, take a moment to breathe and examine the why of the situation. Just as we suggested your children keep an emotion's diary, so too can you as a parent, if you truly want to examine when and why you get upset. Again, this is something you can come together as a family to discuss, once a week, once a month. Whatever you see fit to help you and move you along the path to a higher EQ.

Self-regulation— Manage and control your own emotions! Lead by example and show your kids how it is done. Do not yell or scream at them. Talk to them calmly, coolly. Tell them what is wrong in that relaxed, chill manner of self-regulation. Not a master of self-regulation just yet? Then make it a point to practice being Zen. Admit when you are wrong or have made a mistake to your child, instead of blaming others. Lastly, look at your own values, your code of ethics, and decide what is most important to you as a parent. This will help you make decisions regarding your children as you move through life.

Social skills— Parents with good social skills are open to hearing the good and the bad of life and are great communicators. You can handle changes to your daily schedule, solve problems your little ones might encounter, and set a good example for them to follow. If you are not the best in this area just yet, make a concerted effort to improve your ability to talk to your children about anything and everything. Communication is the key! Remember to praise them for the things they do correctly, even the little things, because this will build their self-esteem, and I cannot stress how important that is. Find a healthy, sane way to solve conflicts in the house and stick with that!

Now, how do these same characteristics affect your children? Let's look at the MESSS once more, but from their perspective: What motivates your child to behave aside from you bribing them with chocolate? Typically it is their love for you. What they want most is your attention, love, and respect. Even if they have a tantrum, try to find one positive thing within that situation. Something you can use to improve that situation in the hopes that it won't happen again. Without empathy our children are lost. Talk to them about how you feel when they don't clean their room, how it hurts your feelings when they don't do their chores, how it is not kind that they don't help around the house with things. Speak to them in the same way you want them to speak to you, and put yourself in their position if you are the one doing the yelling. Help them become self-aware by acknowledging and talking about their emotions with you. Make this a normal and regular thing that you do together. If there is an outburst, breathe and discuss it. Talk about why it happened and what caused it, then find a way to avoid or handle that situation in the future. You should also discuss the self-regulation part of dealing with anger and frustration and the idea of finding a better outlet like primal scream therapy, running, boxing, etc. And finally, their social skills! Communicate with them in a calm and healthy way, and they will learn to communicate with you in that same fashion. It is just that simple!

The Institute for Health and Human Potential actually has an online free test you can take to see how your EQ rates. It's worth completing, so you know where you stand currently. You can find it online at: https://www.ihhp.com/free-eq-quiz/

Benefits of Having a High EQ

If you are able to pull off being an emotionally intelligent parent, then it is very likely that your children will develop this ability as well. Hoorah! Here are some of the many incredibly positive side effects of raising a child with a high EQ.

1. Your child will have a better attention span and will be able to focus on a task much longer without making a fuss.

2. Your child will be the type to self-motivate. Imagine them cleaning their rooms without being asked or doing their homework without you checking on to see if it is done.

3. Your child will handle the ups and downs of life without getting flustered or upset.

4. Your child will be able to control their emotions and not fly off the handle.

5. Did I mention they tend to do better in school? High EQs tend to yield higher IQs!

6. Your child will be much more likely and better equipped to calm themselves down if they get upset, which indubitably will happen because life is a rollercoaster of emotions.

7. Your child will have a higher level of empathy, and they will respect and understand the emotions of other people.

8. Your child will be able to develop stronger and healthier relationships with their friends.

9. Your child can handle difficult situations like bullying and peer pressure because they can respond and connect with others better than those with a lower EQ.

10. Your child will have the ability to recognize and read social cues in different scenarios.

11. Your child will not flip out if you don't give them the chocolate cake right now because they are much better at delaying gratification.

Like most people you might think your child's success in life is based on a high IQ, but what is significantly more important for them is raising their EQ. "While we focus on academic intelligence we often unconsciously minimize the importance of emotional and social intelligence. But studies have shown that only about 20% of what makes people "successful" in life is attributed to their mental intelligence or what they learn in an academic environment. The other 80% is explained by other forces, largely focused on the qualities we describe when we talk about emotional intelligence." [6]

Three of the most common characteristics of successful people reside within the EQ realm: great social skills, a high standard of ethics and integrity, and self-discipline. All three of those qualities center around our ability to understand ourselves and our emotions and then control or manage them so they benefit us or our children.

If you find you are struggling with your own EQ, there are many things that might be getting in your way. Let's face it, if we can't make sense of our own emotions, how are our children going to manage it? The pace of our everyday life certainly makes it difficult to connect with how we really feel. We are so distracted and concerned with ticking off everything on our lengthy to-do list, that emotion falls by the wayside. In my family, we never talked about our feelings, and to this day I find myself writing letters to my mother trying to explain how the things she did (and still does) made (makes) me feel. We carry that stuff with us, whether we want to acknowledge it is there or not, so instead of dealing with it in 30 year's time, try handling these emotions in the here and now.

Do you think you are already an emotionally intelligent parent? Here are five thing that someone with a high EQ would never do:

1. *You do not take your kid's yelling and screaming and acting out personally.* If your little one has a meltdown, rarely is that tantrum about you, so do not take it personally. They are trying to express an emotion, and they simply have not learned the correct way to do it as yet. Take that time to teach them how to handle their emotions, express it nicely, and move past it so you do not have constant eruptions of temperament.

2. _You never ignore the things that upset your little one._ If your child is crying, that means something has upset them. If they tell you something hurt or bothered them, that is how they feel. Pay attention to what those things are. Try writing their emotions down in a journal, when they happened, why they happened, how they expressed themselves. If you truly wish to get to know what bothers your child, and hopefully learn how to avoid those things in the future, this is a great way to do so.

3. _You do not protect them from all of the difficult issues life throws at them._ Your little ones need to learn how to deal with the tough things life will toss at them. It is your job to give them the skills to tackle these hard things and move past them with ease.

4. _You never mock or belittle your child's emotions._ This is something my mother did constantly and still does. If I cried at something hurtful she said, she said I was play acting. My emotions, to this day, count for nothing, and trust me when I say all it does is hurt and belittle your children. It also pushes your kids to hide their feelings away, which has serious nasty side effects for them. Every emotion they have is real and valid to them, and it should be to you as well. If that emotion is unacceptable to the situation, then this is your time to teach them a better way to express their feelings.

5. ***You never try to hide your own emotions from your children.*** Be happy and sing with them. Be sad and cry with them. Be anxious and talk about your fears with them. Tell them about your fear of spiders and ask them what scares them. Be angry (in a healthy way) and do primal scream therapy with them. Show your child that you experience all of the same emotions that they do, but then show them how to handle these emotions and express them correctly. They will be much better off.

We talked about how self-awareness and self-regulation played a big part in your emotional intelligence, and this should reveal how knowing yourself, monitoring yourself, and accepting and discussing all of the good and bad parts of our emotions can help us become much better parents. However, we all reach those breaking point moments, and that's when a little self-care comes in pretty handy. If we don't recharge ourselves, how will we ever effectively face the difficulties involved in caring for others? You won't have anything left to give, and an empty gas tank takes you nowhere. In the next chapter, we will show you how to better take care of you, so you can take better care of your children.

Chapter Summary

• We defined what emotional intelligence (EQ) is.
• We learned the characteristics of emotional intelligence (EQ).
• We learned that having a high EQ could be the most important thing for you and your child.

Chapter Five
Self-Care for Parents

I cannot stress the importance of self-care to you enough! How are you going to be able to care for anybody else if you are tired, malnourished, out of shape, and/or stressed. Clearly, you won't be able to! Take a moment and allow yourself to have some me (you) time. Not giving yourself the time to take care of yourself is doing nobody any favors, so make a note right now to pay attention to what you need so you can be a happier, healthier parent to your child. So many parents think that taking a moment to themselves, going for a run, reading a book, going to an adult film and not the latest Disney film, is self-indulgent, but it is imperative that you carve out moments for yourself where you don't have to be a parent for an hour.

Let me state for the record, your sanity and health are on the line! Both you and your children have essential needs which must be met, so do yourself a huge favor and start paying attention to these aspects of yourself. Self-care is actually anything you do to better your health, and we are not just talking about the physical. According to the National Institute of Mental Illness (NAMI), all self-care habits can be placed into the following six categories:[8]

➔ Professional: Are you happy in your current job? Is it stressful? Do you work crazy hours or have a ridiculously long commute? Do you sit in traffic for hours? Are your coworkers awful? Is your boss a complete buffoon? Are you paid enough? Lots of things contribute to our happiness in our professional lives, so make sure you pay attention to this and see what you can do to improve it.

➔ Spiritual: Are you religious? Do you go to church, temple, or synagogue? Maybe you just believe in karma. However you find satisfaction in your spiritual side, whether it is praying or walking in nature, make sure you take the time to do so.

➔Psychological: Have you been a basket case recently? Do you find yourself getting upset for no reason in particular? Do you find yourself crying or shouting at little things that should be easy to handle? Perhaps you have not been taking care of your mental health. Our minds need just as much care as our bodies, but we seem to forget that for some reason. Take time to talk to a friend, or, if need be, see a therapist to discuss more difficult issues or resolve any serious problems you can't seem to get past on your own.

➜ Physical: When was the last time you worked out? Did you love to ride your bicycle but stopped when you had a child? Did you used to go to spin class religiously? Did you swim laps at the pool every week? Was meeting your friend to play tennis a great way to oust your frustrations and get a work out? Whatever your go-to exercise was, try and reintroduce it into your life. Add a child seat on the back of the bike, strap on a marsupial pouch and go for a walk, take an hour and go to the gym, play that game of tennis with a friend, which would combine healing the physical with the next part—social.

➜ Social: Make time to spend with your friends! If you can't get away, then set up a Facetime call with a glass of wine to catch up with the people you love and miss. Just because you are a parent does not mean the only social interaction you should have is with the little people in your life! You will be amazed how much happier you feel if you do this for yourself. It is so easy to stay connected in this world, so schedule a Facetime call or a WhatsApp video chat, or a Zoom meeting, or a Google chat or whatever social platform you choose if you can't physically meet up, get yourself a glass of wine or make yourself a cocktail and a bowl of popcorn and talk to your friend, or friends. When you don't have the time to get away from the house or your friend lives in a different country, this sort of virtual get together can add a 10, 15, 20 minute blip of joy in your day. Go crazy! Let yourself have an hour! You will see how much better you feel on the back side of a call when you've been laughing with a friend. It makes dealing with your little ones again that much more enjoyable.

➔ Emotional: Time to take care of your own feelings! Did you know that sleep is a huge part of your emotional well being? Making sure you get the proper amount of shut eye is so important to your ability to function mentally and physically. It is also time to learn to say NO to things that are not helpful to your life, because that is a big part of self-care. Stop and breathe deeply before sharing your feelings, and please stop over explaining yourself. You really don't need to do that. For once, put your needs first and let yourself experience whatever it is you are currently feeling.

Self-Care Strategies for Parents

We all have hectic lives, but it is essential to your health to carve out moments for yourself to focus on you and you alone. If you broke your leg, you would go to the doctor and have it taken care of, there would be a cast and some crutches, and time off your feet, well the same should be done for the wellbeing of your psyche. What makes you feel better is something you need to decide, but here are a few things you can try if you are unsure of what might work. Attempt one or two or give all of them a go and see what tickles your fancy:

— Go for a walk in the park, down the street, around the block, through the woods, etc.

— Play your favorite music in the car, on your stereo, on your phone or computer, etc.

— Make sure you have alone time without interruption, even if you just take thirty minutes.

— Splurge on something for yourself as a reward for just trying to be a good parent.

— Try yoga or meditation, something that calms the mind and body and allows you to breathe.

— Start a diary of self-dialogue to express your emotions so they do not get pent up inside.

— Take a bath, get a massage, or have a mani/pedi, whatever makes you feel refreshed.

— Start a garden or get some house plants, grow some vegetables. Digging in the dirt is fun!

— Spend time with your bestie. Meet them for coffee, go for a walk together, go shopping, etc.

– Turn off your phone for an hour so you can unplug from the constant world of notifications.

Teaching Self-Care to Children

No two families are alike, so finding what works for your children might take a little trial and error. That said, just because there is no set in stone guide for self-care, does not mean you can't formulate the perfect one for you and your children. When you start to take care of your own mental and physical health you are showing your little ones the importance of this in their lives and setting them up for greater success in the future.

Explain what self-care is: The term might be new to them, but the things involved in self-care are not. Letting them know that these things are important is something that helps them become better adjusted human beings. "Self-care is just as important as academics for growing, developing kids. When taught correctly, self-care will help kids identify their physical needs and begin to take care of them, before emotions can ever get in the way." [10]

Teach them to take care of their minds and their bodies: There are so many fun ways you can approach these two aspects of self-care with your children. I used to take my daughter to yoga class with me, and she absolutely loved it. She was the youngest one there in the studio, but she was also the most flexible! Getting them into the habit of stretching, breathing, and exercising from a young age will benefit them throughout their lives. But taking care of their bodies does not stop with exercise!

Personal hygiene should also play a big (huge) role in self-care, so make sure you establish good dental habits of floss, brush, rinse that they go through every day after meals, along with washing their hands and bodies, combing their hair, wiping their bums properly from front to back only, cleaning their ears, etc. What about having them help you in the kitchen so they can learn to make healthy foods? That's a great idea! Chop up a salad together or grill some veggies and chicken. Make hummus and eat it with carrots. Teaching them how to do these things will not only hopefully establish a lifelong pattern, but it will also heighten their self-esteem when they see they can do these things themselves. This leads perfectly into the next part of self-care.

Create your healthy family routine: Routines, like the cleaning of the teeth, or set mealtimes, are so important to little ones. It gives them a sense of security and regularity in an otherwise chaotic and unpredictable world. Creating mealtimes, bedtimes, times when they can't use their electronics, time for homework, all of it helps them know what to expect from their day and leads to lower levels of anxiety.

Show them how to have fun away from electronics: Turn off the phones, the computers, the iPads, the video games, and try to find different ways to really connect with your kids. Play outside, enjoy a board game or cards, read a book together, write a poem, paint a picture, cook something fun together, teach them to knit or craft or swim or whatever it is you enjoy. Share that with them and connect in a meaningful way. My daughter used to love to make homemade hot pretzels. We would make the dough, roll it out, shape the pretzels, laugh, get flour all over ourselves, and then eat our creations. It is something, even at the age of 17, she still wants to do with me.

My self-care ritual was lighting scented candles, making myself a bubble bath, bringing in a glass of wine, a plate of sushi, and my phone. I would eat, drink, relax, and call a friend all in one go, getting in quite a few of my self-care items, and then emerge feeling like a new person. Take time out to treat yourself to these little you moments, and you will see you return to parenting feeling calmer, more refreshed, and ready to go another couple of rounds.

As we have stated throughout the book so far, every family is different, so make a self-care plan that is right for you and your children, and then make a daily routine that is right for you and your children. Look for things you can do alongside your little ones that promote everyone's physical and mental health. Not only will it bond you as a family, but it will help them create beneficial habits that can last for a lifetime. In the next chapter, we will help you figure out and identify which type of parenting style you currently use and provide other options in case you need to try something new.

Chapter Summary

- We learned the importance of self-care.
- We learned what you can do to improve your own self-care routine.
- We learned how to teach self-care to our children.

Chapter Six
Parenting Styles

What type of parent are you? I don't mean are you a good parent or are you a bad parent. I'm wondering what type of parenting style you currently use to discipline your children? These days all we hear about in the press are helicopter parents, lawnmower parents, koala mums, lighthouse parents, and drone parents, but these are all new styles that developed only recently. There are actually four main styles that were created way back in the 60s to describe a few of the most common approaches to raising children. As well we know, this is not a one size fits all type of thing, and as you read on you might realize that your approach combines different aspects from the various types of parenting styles. If that is what you do, then that means you can give your style its own cool name!

Four Types of Parenting Styles

Authoritative: This style of parenting is thought to be the healthiest because it is one in which you communicate clearly with your child and have reasonable expectations that coincide with your kid's age. Doesn't that sound sensible? You are a caring, loving parent and in return your children tend to be self-motivated and discipline themselves. Imagine that! Children that are prone to self-discipline! They do exist. I have one of those unicorns living under my roof, but I owe that to using this type of parenting style. Thanks to your evolved levels of communication, your little ones understand what you want from them and can easily discuss their issues with you sans fear. They are not afraid you are going to start screaming at them for any little thing. An authoritative parent discusses issues rationally, calmly, and regularly, and that is a beautiful thing for everyone.

Authoritarian: The authoritarian parent, otherwise known as the disciplinarian style of parenting is quite rigid. You are the mother or father who is quite strict and quick to punish with the lines of communication typically running only in one direction—from you to your child. What they have to say is not important to you, and you just don't want to hear it. You don't really give them a chance to explain, nor do you care to hear any excuses or explanations. You are a "because I said so" type of parent, quite like mine was. Did I mention you also have incredibly high expectations from your children which are almost impossible for them to meet? This sets them up for failure, over and over again, which, in turn, lowers their self-esteem, creating further issues for both of you. The authoritarian does not explain to their child why they want things the way they do, but they certainly expect them to be that way!

Permissive: This is the type of parent that likes to consider themselves their child's best friend, not their child's disciplinary figure. Like the uninvolved parent, they let their kid do what they want, but in this case it is because they want to make them happy. If you have taken on this style of parenting, you communicate warmly with your children, but you don't really offer them guidance or discipline, and you certainly don't set down any expectations for their behavior or academics. You generally get along well with your children and are loving and caring, but again more as a pal than a parent. This can lead to your children getting into trouble in school and out because you haven't given them any guidelines to live by or rules to follow or goals to meet.

Uninvolved: This is what I like to call the non-parenting style of parenting. You basically let your child do what they want because you don't really care or you don't have the time to participate in their lives. Sometimes, this happens because a single parent has to work all of the time, and in those cases it is sad because it does cause harm to the child. Other times, it is just because a parent could care less what their kids are doing, and that is also sad, but in a very different way. Unfortunately, there is not much in the way of love, attention, or communication from the uninvolved style of parenting, and these children often run wild and do whatever the heck they want which generally leads to trouble.

Parenting styles are subject to fads, and recently there has been an uptick in the discussion of helicopter parenting. This is the type of parent that is overly protective and overly involved in everything their children do. They like to hover like a helicopter, constantly watching and interfering in the life of their kids. In addition, slow parenting is also having a moment, thanks to the hectic nature of most of our lives, wherein people are making a concerted effort to decelerate the speed of their day to day to try and be better parents. In some privileged circles, parenting has become a competitive sport, but what you really need to remember, despite the style you currently use, the needs for healthy child development remain relatively simple: safety, structure, support, and love. If you can give your child those four things, the style is inconsequential.

Why Parenting Styles Matter

Unhealthy parenting can come in many forms from many styles, because not every parenting style is in a child's best interest. Let's take a look at some of the downsides these styles can have on your child. There is such a thing as over parenting, like in helicopter parenting, which can cripple children as they move into adulthood and render them unable to cope with the merest setbacks because you have done everything for them, and then they can do nothing for themselves. We have to teach our children to handle situations, to grow, and to be able to take care of themselves.

Being an authoritarian parent might give you a child that currently obeys, but at the end of the day that little one will most likely become angry at you, resent you, and then become aggressive with others. Sadly, they will suffer from low self-esteem because you never listened to them or valued anything they had to say. Oftentimes, the children of authoritarian parents are adept liars because they were so tired of having their parents yell at them they resorted to fibbing their way out of a sticky situation.

That permissive parenting style you adopted might give you a child who thinks you're cool, but it just as easily might give you a child who overeats because you aren't telling them not to! They also have a tendency to suffer from lower grades, lower self-esteem, and an inability to follow rules because, whoopsie, you never set any for them!

Lastly, the uninvolved parent is bound to have a lonely child with low self-esteem, and one who does not do well or behave themselves in school. Not that you would know, because you are not involved.

If, however, you find yourself currently using the authoritative style of parenting, then congratulations! Your child is more likely to be both happy and successful and grow up to be a responsible adult. Imagine that! It can be done!

Effects on Your Children

Your parenting style can affect everything from how much your child weighs and what grades they get in school to how they feel about themselves now and how they will feel about themselves as adults. It is so important to ensure that your parenting style is supporting the healthy growth and development of your little ones. My mother most definitely used an authoritarian style of parenting. She would have her rules, which, if broken, were met with the wooden spoon and then the dread cry of, "Now go sit on the stairs and think about what you have done!" I was never sure which part of that punishment was worse, the physical whacks or the mental torture as I sat there thinking about how horrid I was.

There was never any discussion about what she wanted or why she wanted it that way, it was always just her way or you got into serious trouble. Her actions and behavior and parenting style led me to suffer through issues of low self-esteem because as children we believe, if our parents can't love us, how can anyone else and what's wrong with me? The temperament of your child is shaped by you. The mental health of your child is shaped by you. Their ability to cope with all of life's situations is shaped by you. That is why we must do everything we can to control our anger, find a better way to react to our kids being naughty, come from a place of calm instead of having a knee jerk reaction, and be able to discipline in a smooth and benevolent manner.

Of course, children need structure and discipline, but how you go about imposing it will have lasting effects on them. There is a right way, a nice way, a kind way to get them to behave, one that does not involve raising your voice. Think about that the next time you have to correct your little one's behavior. Now that you are aware of these different styles and their pros and cons you can decide what would most benefit your kids at this moment. We all want to do what is best for our children, you would not be reading this book if you did not, and in the next chapter we will go over a few positive parenting tips to help you succeed in doing just that.

Chapter Summary

- We learned about the four main parenting styles.
- We learned why these parenting styles matter.
- We learned the positive and negative effects these styles can have on your children.

Chapter Seven
Positive Parenting Tips

Don't we all want to be the cheerleaders in our children's lives? I dreamt of being this supportive, helpful, loving parent that helped my child reach their goals and built their self-esteem instead of cutting it down faster than a Brazilian rainforest. I wanted to teach my child right from wrong, have an open line of communication, and a mutual respect for one another, one where I would be showing my child how to control themselves appropriately in all different situations. Enter, positive parenting!

There are a few main ideas in positive parenting that make it function successfully, and to me these things just make sense. They really do! The rules and punishments you make for your children are talked about, their existence explained, they are changed when necessary, and all of it is done openly with your children so everyone knows the what, the when, the why and the how. Nothing is a surprise. In positive parenting, you are taught to never try to discipline your child when you yourself are not calm and in complete control of your words and your own mind!

Make sure you breathe and find a little Zen before you dole out the discipline! You help your little ones create and maintain self-discipline, and you listen to what they have to say when they explain why they did things so you can correct and steer them away from any bad logic before they go further down that trail. If you have to hand out a dose of discipline, make sure you calmly talk about why they are being punished and then reconnect with your child afterwards by doing something together that bonds you and shows them that you still love them.

Positive parenting is all about rewarding and noticing their good actions instead of only giving them attention when they are naughty. Remember to set realistic expectations for their age and take care of yourself too with some of that self-care we talked about so you have the right frame of mind to be calm and positive with your little ones. Positive parenting is all about sharing what you think and feel and believe with your children.

Benefits of Positive Parenting

There are many benefits for you and your children when you use a positive parenting method to raise them. It is all about creating a warm and nurturing environment where they can grow and mature. Think of them like a plant. Each one might need a little different level of light or nutrients, and in this case love and guidance, encouragement and acceptance from you (they all need nutrients!). One of the most important things positive parenting does is create a loving, caring relationship between you and your little ones, and that is something we all strive for as parents.

Some of the benefits of positive parenting:

— Improves the line of communication between you and your children. Being able to talk to your kids with ease is a magical thing!

— Reduces the frequency of naughty behavior. (Wouldn't that be a refreshing change?)

— Builds a shared level of respect between you and your child.

— Raises your children's self-esteem and confidence levels because you talk to them and value their opinions and feelings as much as your own.

— It shows children how to behave in a positive way because you have been a great example for them to replicate.

— It gives you a much stronger bond to your little ones, and as much as they need and want us to love them, we also need and want them to love us.

— It really teaches your kids how to make smart decisions including how to behave in different settings and scenarios. Life is going to throw things at them, and this way they are prepared!

— It shows them how to maintain control of their emotions, and not be ruled by them. Back to the Janet Jackson mantra here!

— Teaches your children respect for others because you have shown respect to them and for them. This is moving into Aretha Franklin's territory, but the woman was not wrong when she sang about how much she wanted R E S P E C T!

— Because they have learned to communicate well with you, they will be able to communicate on a higher level with others which generates better friendships and ease with relationships.

Studies have absolutely proven the high number of benefits for both parent and child when you use a positive parenting style. A research paper published in the Journal of Clinical Adolescent Psychology showed that using a positive parenting style gave a child a greatly decreased chance of suffering from depression when it was compared to more severe parenting styles like the authoritarian approach. That same study also revealed that adults who had suffered through a more militant style of parenting when they were kids had a far greater frequency of mental health problems like depression when they were grown up, and they were also likely to hand those issues down to their kids. Time to break the cycle, become a positive parent, and let that positivity affect future generations of your family in a good way!

Challenges of Positive Parenting

One negative aspect of positive parenting that is wise to pay attention to is that your children won't learn how to deal with the nasty or negative parts of life if you are always positive. There are moments in life where we are bound to get annoyed. We get upset and take our anger out on someone when we should not, and this is just part of normal, everyday life. Nobody is perfect! So, the one part of positive parenting you need to watch out for is this, even though you do give mostly affirming attention you still need to train your children how to deal with negative reactions. They might not get them at home, but they will definitely encounter them in the outside world. It is your job to make sure they are adequately prepared to handle them. Someone is going to yell at them. Someone is going to scream at them, and they need to be ready to deal with that. Talk openly with your children about fears and anxieties, because even those things fall under negative emotions. This will give your kids a more well balanced perspective. Another factor that might hinder you from always being a positive parent—life! Sometimes we are so overworked, stressed, and exhausted that it is impossible to go to that happy place and be calm when our children are acting up. Please, don't beat yourself up! Nobody can be positive all of the time unless they are highly medicated.

Essential Positive Parenting Tips by Age Group

What your child will need from you to continue to develop in a healthy, happy manner will change over time as they grow from baby to toddler to teen, but you might be surprised to know there are quite a few things that stay the same.

— Love them.

— Pay attention to them.

— Respect them and their opinions.

— Spend time with them.

Acknowledge and reward their good behaviors more often than you punish them for their bad ones. Encourage them to read, to respect others, to be kind, and to be thoughtful. Help your little ones make good decisions and remember to laud them when they do. This is part of rewarding and acknowledging their good behavior. Get to know their friends, their interests, and their passions. Talk to them regularly and make sure the lines of communication are always open. They need to feel they can come to you to discuss things, even when they make mistakes... actually, especially when they make mistakes. If you can do most or all of these things, then you are well on your way. Positive parenting is right around the corner!

(0-1) This is the time to sing, talk, and read to your child in the way you would speak to another adult. None of that baby talk! This is the time they need to develop their communication skills. Let them hear you and get to know your voice and that alone will make them happy. Watch them smile when you say their name or sing to them. Cuddle your baby as much as you can and play with them when they are awake. Answer your baby if they are calling for you. This makes them feel safe and loved. Even though this is a hectic time filled with so much to do for them, you need to make sure you also take good care of yourself, get enough rest, eat healthy foods, and get in some exercise. Remember to bring in that self-care we talked about previously!

(1-2) Respond positively and often to your child's good behavior instead of only noticing and punishing their bad behavior. If they think you only pay attention when they are naughty, you are setting yourself up to perpetuate their

bad behavior. Keep on reading to your children daily. Talk to them like an adult (not in baby language) correcting their words so you can help them develop their vocabulary. You can assist them along the road to independence by letting them choose their clothes or feed themselves.

(2-3) Teach your child appropriate ways to show they are upset. They will get angry and annoyed, but show them how to relay those feelings in a kinder, gentler way. Focus on giving them love and attention and reward them when they follow directions or do what they are supposed to, instead of just giving them negative attention when they are naughty. Share some songs you can sing together and help them identify themselves by name and age. And please keep reading to them!

(3-5) If you tell your child NO, make sure you then explain what you do want from them instead. If they get upset, please help them find a solution to whatever is bothering them. Keep speaking to them like an adult and correct their words if they make mistakes. This will continue to improve and expand their vocabulary. Do some simple tasks around the house together like sweeping or cleaning so they feel like they are helping. Sharing is caring was a big rule in my house, and one we repeated whenever the occasion warranted. It rhymes and it stays with them. Keep reading and take them to a book shop or a library to further

advance their love of the written word.

(6-8) Please hug and kiss your child! This is so very important. It sounds like a given, but it is not. I cannot stress this to you enough—give them your attention, time, and care! Show your little ones they are loved and very much cherished. Also, recognize and extoll their accomplishments. They need to hear your praise as it matters more than anyone else's. Talk to your child about everything: life, school, other kids, their goals for the future, how to be kind, discuss the importance of helping others, and then talk to them some more. Keeping that line of communication wide open from a young age will matter even more in the future. Develop their patience by getting them to wait for things they want, perhaps let a sibling or friend go on the swing first and encourage this behavior with affection and kind words and a treat. Define to your children which behaviors are acceptable and which are not and lay out what punishments will come if they disobey. Make sure you follow through on that discipline when necessary. Enjoy some fun family activities together. This will bond you! Again, remember to praise their good behavior and keep reading!

(9-11) At this age, it is time to discuss things like spending money wisely, the importance of helping others, and the fun of puberty, which is just around the corner. It

is also wise to meet the parents of your child's friends. You should know what sort of influence they might have and what type of environment your children might be spending time in. Encourage them to set goals and discuss what things they want to learn. Set aside special parent/child time where you can encourage them to join teams or groups or do volunteer work. Discuss peer pressures they might face at this age and how they can deal with them. Remember to be loving and kind and honest, and do things together as a family to continue to strengthen that bond. Lastly, remember to encourage them to keep on reading!

(12-14) If you have not already, make sure you learn who your child's friends are and get to know them and their parents, especially as they make new friends. Always remember to listen to your teenager. Let them know you love and respect them and value their opinions and feelings. Talk honestly and openly about things like alcohol, drugs and, sex with them so they can make informed and healthy choices or if they get into trouble they feel comfortable coming to you for solutions. If there is an issue, which there will be, allow your teen to offer some possible solutions. It will make them feel like they are contributing and that you value their input. It doesn't have to be right, but you do have to listen and not outright shoot down their ideas. Try something like, "that's a good idea, and I appreciate what

you are saying, but it might be better to do," insert whatever you believe it is that will work best.

(15-17) Here is a tough one, but let's try and respect your teen's need for privacy. There will be lots of new developments at this stage with their bodies, with their hormones, with their social life, so give them space, but make sure they know you are there for them. Get them to try volunteer work, or if they have a job you can discuss how to save money, deal with the public, and respect their coworkers. Make sure they are getting an appropriate amount of exercise and sleep, and that they are eating nutritious foods. Run through scenarios they might encounter as a teen, including sexual issues, drug and alcohol related problems, drunk driving scenarios, etc. and how they can best handle all of those situations. Love them, hug them, and spend quality time together doing things that make you both happy. Remember to laud their accomplishments. Talk to them often and watch out for any shifts in their behavior. This can be a sign that something is wrong.

Throughout this chapter, we have explored the benefits that learning and adopting a positive parenting style can have on you and your entire family. There are so many wonderful aspects of this approach that just make sense when you stop and think about them. Even if you have not been the calmest, most available or communicative parent thus far, it is never too late to change your ways, but the faster you implement these ideas the easier it is for everyone to grow and flourish within the family circle.

A few months ago I was talking to my sister, and we were trying to remember something we did with our mother that was fun, a happy moment, where we shared some laughs with her. Both of us had to really dig for something. I said blueberry picking, to which she replied, "You disappeared with your bucket and returned with a blue face and a stomach ache. The only reason you think it was a fun memory is because you loved blueberries and she drove us there, but you never spoke to her while you were picking."

Then I brought up the time she rented a beach house for a week. She said, "We played all day with our cousins and never saw her until meal times. Again, it was nothing we did together. She just brought us there. That was the week she divorced our father. Remember, she disappeared for a day?"

I did not recall that part of the holiday. What made me so sad was the fact that I didn't really have one truly happy shared moment of us doing something together. She was always working or disciplining, and I understand the working part, but I make sure to create many happy shared moments with my child. This way, she won't have to wrack her brain for one, instead she will have to think, which one!

Most of the efforts I have made to become a good parent sprang from the fact that my mother was not. I did not want to have a similar relationship with my child. I could never talk to my mother about anything, and she never made you feel welcome to come to her if you had problems. Most of the improvements I have made in my own relationship with my child come from committing to always have open and honest communication with them, which is what we will cover in the next chapter.

Chapter Summary

- We learned what positive parenting is and why it is so important.
- We discussed what issues might arise from positive parenting and how to avoid them.
- We discussed positive parenting tips to use for all ages of your child's development.

Chapter Eight
Effective Communication

Do you find it difficult to talk to your children? Don't worry! You are not alone. Many parents do, but this is something that is so important to having a healthy and happy relationship with your child. If chatting with your child is not an issue, then congratulations! But, if it is something you currently struggle with, have no fear. There are lots of ways to improve upon this skill and open up the lines of communication between you and your kids, and this chapter will offer you some tips and strategies to help you do just that. Talking to your little ones makes them feel special and important, and all good parents want their children to feel both of those things. Showing them how to talk openly with you, will also give them a helpful skill they can use for the rest of their lives because they will be better able to communicate with others. Again, every child is different and so is every parent, and what works for one might not work for another, so find the method that best functions for you and your family.

Strengthening the Parent Child Bond

Creating a strong bond with your child is what is going to get you through the rough patches that every relationship is bound to face at some point or another. Life does not always make it easy to get along perfectly with our children, but if you keep trying and don't give up you can create a strong and secure connection between you and your child that won't break.

1. *Make sure you show your little one how much you love them!* Never underestimate how important your love and affection are to your child at any and all ages. In my house, I started to say to my child, "it looks like your hug-o-meter is low," and proceeded to give out the most heart-warming, intense hug. Soon enough, when my child saw me a bit sad or just because, they would return the embrace to raise up the level of my hug-o-meter. It is something we still do now when they are 17 years old. A loving touch or hug or caress or kiss several times a day is needed to keep this bond intact and allow them to feel connected to you. Any time you see your little one, even if you are just passing through the living room, smile at them, grab their hand and give it an affectionate squeeze, but honestly connect and build this feeling of love between you.

2. *Understand how important it is to listen to your child and identify with them.* You won't know what is going on in your children's lives or within their emotions if you do not listen to what they have to say and make an effort to understand what it is they are saying . It is up to you to make them feel comfortable coming to you about things—any things, bad things, good things, ugly things, uncomfortable things. You really need them to tell you all of it. Nod your head as they talk, look in their eyes, touch their hand, don't get upset, and show them you are there for them and you are listening intently to every word they say. Empathizing with their highs and lows in life will bond you even further. Try and see things from their perspective and let them know that you are there to listen and help with whatever they need.

3. *If you really want to talk to your children, they need your undivided attention.* Have you ever tried to have a conversation with someone that was not really listening to you? It is beyond impossible and very rude. So, put down the phones, turn off the TV, and talk to your children. Maybe make dinner the time you come together as a family to chat about things. You can also tell your kids if they have something they want to talk about in private that you always have time, perhaps when they are going to bed. Tuck them in, sit beside them, snuggle with them and talk. No matter how old they are, this is always a lovely ritual to go through each night. These little ones need to be assured that even with all of life's hectic messiness, they are your number one priority, and you always have time for them.

4. ***Make sure to create and discuss your family's list of rights and wrongs and punishments.*** Your little munchkins are going to need some rules to live by, and these need to be set up and discussed in advance. Sitting down together as a family and going over the rules of the house is important to maintaining that line of communication. Your children need to know what will happen if they break a house rule, and if they do you need to enforce the established punishment, otherwise the system will not work. As your kids grow, rules and punishments can and should change, which is why I suggest using meal time to keep this an ongoing dialogue between you and your children. You can talk about what is fair and come to an agreement together about the consequences they might suffer if a rule gets broken. There should be no surprises in discipline.

If they know in advance what you expect them to do and how you expect them to act and behave, and they know what will happen if they do not, then there is no shock or disconnect when a punishment is given. You can have everyone agree that these are the house rules and this is the fair punishment for breaking them. Involving them in establishing set discipline is a great thing to keep you all connected on and on the same page. If you do have to dish out a giant helping of discipline, make sure you reestablish your connection with your disobedient child by taking them and doing something together that is enjoyable. Use that time to talk about what they did wrong and how they can avoid doing that in the future. Don't forget to remind them how much you love them, and that you just want them to be the best me I can be!

5. *Take some time and be a kid again!* When was the last time you played with your child? Go fishing, go for a bicycle ride, go for a hike, put on a play, go get your nails done, just go do something fun together. Whatever makes you laugh and enjoy each other's company. There are many things that playtime teaches your children: how to relate to others, how to better communicate, not only with words but also emotions, how to be creative, and how to better socialize with others. On top of all of that, you can use playtime to simply bond with your children. Laughing with them and having fun is what is most important. It doesn't really matter what you do, as long as you are both enjoying it and enjoying each other's company.

6. *Relax and just enjoy the moment!* We all know how hectic life can be, but sometimes you just need to chill out and enjoy whatever is happening right now. Don't think about tomorrow or what's for dinner, turn off your phone and spend some quality time with your child.

7. *Spend some ongoing quality time with your child.* Every Sunday my little one and I would go to the pool for a swim at night. It was our Sunday ritual, and one we enjoyed together. She would always look forward to that time when we were alone. These scheduled, routine moments are very important to establish with your kids. You can set up different activities for each child to make those shared moments special and distinct. This time will do nothing but strengthen the parent-child bond, and show them how much you love, value, and care about them. These moments together also build your child's self-esteem. Make it something you both really enjoy doing together that way it is a win-win for the both of you.

8. *Sit down and have your meals as a family.* The family that eats together, bonds together! This is the time to talk, all of you, together, as a family. Phones should be off or far away, and the focus should be on talking to one another about anything and everything that is going on. Talk about your feelings, say what the high and low points of your day were, what your favorite part of the meal is, what is not working in the house as far as discipline or chores, just talk and enjoy this time together. What you are eating is also important, because within these meals you can teach your kids the value of eating healthy, balanced meals. Teach them about the food pyramid and what foods are nutritious. Don't let them eat a lot of junk, drink soda, or snack on candy. Instead, give them hummus and carrot sticks, get them to drink plenty of water, and try fruit or air popped organic corn. This is something that will not only help them grow, but also keep them healthy for the rest of their lives. They grow up all too quickly, so relish in these family meals while you still can.

9. *Most importantly, tell them you love them every day!* If you are looking for things that affect your relationship with your little one, look no further than the words I love you. You might think that they know this, but guess what, they usually don't get tired of hearing it and most of them need a reminder. Especially after you have had to discipline them about something! Be sure to take a moment to reconnect yourself with your child and remind them that you do and will always love them. It boosts their self-esteem and further bonds the two of you, so write it on a note and stick it on their pillow, tell them when they leave for school, remind them again when they are going to sleep.

If there is one thing that keeps people bonded, it is love.

Tips and Strategies to Improve Communication

Let's go through some various strategies to help you improve those currently stilted or nonexistent chats with your kids. They might be rough or awkward at the moment, but there are many things you can do to fix that. Put yourself in their shoes, they want to talk to you, but sometimes they just don't know how to go about it. Remember, it is your job to make it easy for them to approach you with their problems, their worries, their troubles and fears, as well as their good news. Don't you want them coming to you for advice instead of going to someone else?

Here are a few tips to improve the art of communication:

● Make sure you speak to them with respect and keep everything polite.

● You can be the one to open up the conversation. Start with a question they will have to answer. Try asking about their day! That's an easy one that always has a reply.

● Make sure you take turns listening and talking. A good conversation is not one sided!

● Get your child's attention the right way. Don't barge into their room or verbally attack them. Approach calmly and start with a "pardon me" or "are you busy right now?" to get the verbal ball rolling in the right direction.

● Make sure you know when you should stop talking and let them be the one to speak.

● Always maintain eye contact with your child.

● Praise your child whenever they are polite and use their communication skills well! This will push them to repeat these behaviors because more than anything they really want to please you.

Ironically, the best thing you can do to improve communication with your children is to listen, and I mean really listen, using something called active listening, which is a skill you can acquire easily if you do not already possess it. Active listeners do many of the following things:

● You can help your child express their feelings by offering up a possible emotion. "That must have hurt when your sister did not ask you to do the puzzle with her." Don't worry if you are wrong because this opens the door for them to explain how they really feel.

● Pay attention to your little one's body language and what their face is telling you. Being a great listener is not only about hearing the words that come out of their mouths.

● Show you are really listening by saying their own words back to them. This tells your little ones you are hearing what they are saying. "I didn't have fun at the party, mom!" "I'm sorry to hear you didn't have fun at the party! What happened?"

● Cultivate excitement in their words and show you are interested by saying things like: Oh, wow! How did that happen? What happened next? Go on! Tell me more!

● Listen to them first and don't offer any opinions. They might just need someone to hear their thoughts or feelings. Then, after they have finished, ask them if they want to know how you would handle that situation or offer to help them, but don't push in on their talking time. That is rude and not helpful.

● If your little one is having difficulty expressing themselves, try really hard not to talk over them, or interrupt, or worse yet finish their sentences. Instead, prompt them to continue or simply ask your child a question if you don't understand.

● Show them you are listening not just with words, but also with your body. Turn off your phone, or at least put it away, look at them, hold their hand, or snuggle. This is an intimate time to share and really connect with your child.

Talking with Babies

Okay, we know they can't ask you what's for dinner,

but from the moment they are born your little ones do make all sorts of noises. These sounds are their way of speaking to you. Granted, they will cry quite a bit too, but that noise means all sorts of things to them. It is your job to determine what they are saying. Try talking to them as you would an adult and pause to allow them to answer. You might be surprised to find they will coo and gurgle during those moments of silence. Keep having these conversations with them on a daily basis and watch how their communication skills grow.

Talking with Preschoolers

Preschool children ages three to five are the chattiest bunch because at this point they are learning to develop their social skills. Some fun ways to communicate with them might be through rhyming, reading, or singing. Remember, it does not have to be kid's music that makes them happy. My child loved "Mr. Cab Driver" by Lenny Kravitz and would ask to hear it every time we got in the car. To this day we still sing it together and feel that same joyful bond. These connections and moments of togetherness matter now and in the long run.

Your children feel a constant need to talk and ask questions, so do your best to answer them using adult language. Do not talk down to them or use baby talk because they are learning their vocabulary from you and will think this is how adults speak. These little ones will also communicate with you through gestures and sounds, crafting, and make believe.

Play out different scenarios together. You remember what it was like! Pretend phone calls! Pretend going to the market! Pretend ordering at a restaurant! Join in! Be a kid again! All of this play acting helps your little ones develop those social skills.

This is also the time to make sure they are being polite. Make sure the please and thank you portion of their vocabulary is on point! Now is also the time to teach them that interrupting is not polite. You can show them alternatives, like touching you on the arm when you are speaking if they need to get your attention. Do it with kindness. Do it with love, but teach them to be both kind and polite.

Talking with School Age Children

Your child will learn their conversation skills from you, and for this reason you can help them develop how they communicate. First off, ask them about school! Ask them how their day was, what did they learn, have they made any new friends, what is their favorite class or teacher. School will be their life, so make sure they know you are interested in it. Have conversations with your children and take turns listening and asking questions and answering. Remind them to look at the person they are talking to, and if they forget "please and thank you," prompt them quickly to add it to whatever they were saying. Hopefully by this age they don't need reminding, but make sure these things stick. You can help them with conversations by guiding them in what they might say. For example: Your cousin just got a new dog. I'm sure they'd love it if you called to find out more about the animal. If they are hesitant to meet new people, run through an introduction with them until they feel comfortable saying it on their own.

If they are still interrupting, which I hope they aren't, tell them they have to wait until you are finished speaking and then say "excuse me" and wait until you answer. Continue to praise them when they are communicating with you the right way. Thank them for not interrupting. Commend them for holding the door open or helping bring in the groceries or always remembering to say please and thank you. Our jobs as parents revolve around our ability to shape a well-mannered individual who can communicate correctly in polite society.

Talking with Pre Teens

When children move into their teenage years, typically friends become the most important thing in their lives. This does not mean they don't need you, in fact it is when they need to know they have your complete love and support, even if the last thing they would do is tell you so. Just because they want more independence and privacy does not mean they don't need you. Our role as a parent is now to keep monitoring their behavior, offer them advice when it is needed, and continue to support and love them. This might be the time we want to discuss the issue of back talking. Sassy children are out there, so don't let yours be one of them. Here are some things you can do to deter them from this type of rude behavior:

● Even if what they say is hilarious, do not laugh! This will only encourage them to keep talking back to you. We must avoid rewarding negative behavior at all costs.

● If for some reason, your child continues to be sassy, make sure there is some sort of repercussion for the behavior—take away that phone or video game they love so much.

● Show them another, nicer, more polite way to respond, but do it in a calm way. Do not yell. Remember, you are trying to teach them to be polite, so, in that sense, and always, so too should you.

● It might be smart to establish some family rules about speaking politely not just between parent and child, but also between siblings. Discuss and define these rules together as a family so everyone is on the same page and set down what sort of repercussions will happen if they break your guidelines of politeness.

Get to know your children's friends now! You will be thankful you did. Be aware that these friendships can sometimes lead to problems when they go from friend to enemy, the dreaded frenemy, in the course of a day. Friendships change, sometimes they go sour, and having you there to help them, to be their unshifting rock, will be helpful now and well into their teenage years.

Talking with Teens

You remember what it was like to be a teenager, don't you? Make sure you stay connected to your children during this generally tumultuous time in their lives. Use everyday moments to chat with them and express your interest in how they are doing, what they are doing, physically and emotionally. Have them help you make dinner and use that time to find out what is going on in their lives. Whether it is unplanned or scheduled time, make sure you have these moments of communication. Use enjoyable family trips or outings and daily things like dinner time to come together and connect.

You can also plan one-on-one time with your teen, maybe go do something they enjoy together or try something new together like a pottery class that will give you an opportunity to chat. Use those active listening skills and don't interrupt them while they are speaking, give them your undivided attention, don't chastise or judge them, and remain calm. Active listening is going to tell your child they are the most important things in the world to you at this moment. Remember, they might be teens, but they still need hugs and love from you, even if they now have a boyfriend or girlfriend. Just don't forget to knock on their bedroom door before you enter! They do like and appreciate a bit of privacy at this point.

The teen years will bring about a lot of the most difficult conversations, but don't shy away from them. Hopefully, by this point you have a strong and healthy line of communication built up between you, and this will make those talks that much easier. Discussing things like sex with your kids might be uncomfortable, but you will both survive. Try and make it as relaxed as possible. That way, when you approach topics like drugs and liquor use, their sexual orientations, mental health, money, career goals and work, any issues they might be having at school, masturbating, etc. they feel comfortable enough to talk about all of these things with you. When you plow through these tough talks cooperating as a team this is a very good sign. It means you have a great relationship with your child. Dealing with the rough stuff together will simply make them feel closer to you.

Here are a few practical tips for dealing with the dicey topics:

● Practice that active listening! You should be a pro by now.

● Just stay calm! Do not go in frazzled! Prepare what you want to say ahead of time and do not lose your temper or raise your voice.

● Do not under any circumstance become overly emotional. Do not judge and do not criticize them! This will make them never want to tell you things. You have to make this a warm, welcoming, non judgemental, and comfortable space for them to share their thoughts. Tell them how happy you are that they want to discuss these things with you and to always do so in the future whenever they have a problem.

● Tell them that you do indeed want to talk to them about whatever is bothering them or, better yet, that you want to have a discussion with them about sex or drugs or alcohol before there are any issues.

If, for some reason, talking face to face is too difficult for your teen (or for you) there are other means of communication to explore including written letters, email, or even text messages. Just remember the outright importance of communicating with your kids. It is a horrible feeling for a child when they think they can't talk to you or that you don't really care what they are feeling or thinking. In the next chapter, we will discuss what to do when you are just too far over your head and need some help with the job of being a parent.

Chapter Summary

- We discussed the importance of effective communication.
- We showed you how to strengthen the parent-child bond.
- We gave you tips to improve your communication skills.

Chapter Nine
Parent Therapy

We all know that the job of being a good parent is not an easy one, and it is not a task to take on lightly or treat like a part time job. Being a good parent is an ongoing process where you and your child learn alongside each other what works for your lives so both parties can flourish and then do their best. As hard as we try on our own, sometimes personal attempts are just not enough, and you can feel yourself drowning in the role. Luckily, there are many options available that can act as parenting lifelines. Sure, going out for a drink with our other friends that are also parents can give us a boost, but they aren't always the best source of advice or a long term solution. That friend will provide a person to vent to, and probably a few laughs, which helps in many ways, but if you are still feeling overwhelmed it might be time to look into something more, like family therapy, one on one therapy, parenting classes, or a parenting group.

Parenting Classes and Parenting Groups

For many, the decision to work with a counselor or therapist is the best parenting decision they have ever made. Simply put, a parenting class is a course you can take that teaches you how to be a good parent. Just like you would take Spanish class if you wanted to learn that language, taking a parenting class to learn a new skill is quite logical. We aren't born knowing how to be great parents. The classes are used to help you improve your homelife by showing you the ropes of how to juggle caring for your domicile, yourself, and your kids and to simply improve the relationship you have with your children. Nothing wrong with that!

Benefits of Parenting Classes

— You can learn what to expect as your child grows and develops so you are better prepared.

— You can learn how to identify your own parenting strengths and how best to use them to their potential.

— You can learn how to handle any major issues that might arise.

— You can learn how to best discipline your children, not use anger based reactions, and what is an age appropriate method to fix any naughty behavior.

— If you have been divorced or are going through a divorce, these classes can help you and your ex learn how to work together to provide a healthy and happy homelife for your children amidst this changing environment.

— If you have remarried and combined families or are in the process, this is a great place to learn how to do so in a way that will be easier for everyone involved.

In addition to actual in room sessions, there are many online parenting classes available, and these are typically less expensive, in case you are working on a budget. A quick online search for what your specific needs are should give you several options to choose from. The best online family classes in 2021 were [19]:

● The Best Overall Class: <u>Megan Leahy Parent Coach</u>

● The Best for Decision-Making: <u>The Science of Parenting</u>

● The Best in Dollar Value: <u>Peace at Home Parenting Solutions</u>

● The Best for Dealing with Power Struggles: <u>Positive Parenting Solutions</u>

● The Best for Co-Parenting: <u>Crossroads of Parenting and Divorce by Active Parenting</u>

● The Best for Organizing: <u>The Unfrazzled Mom by Messy Motherhood</u>

● The Best for Managing Stress: <u>Peaceful Parent, Happy Kids by Aha! Parenting</u>

Parenting Groups

What is a parenting group, you might ask. Typically, it is a group of families that come together to help each other solve similar problems they all might be facing, reaffirming the adage that two heads are better than one. In this case, multiple heads are better than one! It is also a way for your family to meet other families and engage in some socialization. Many of these groups are also online, but it still offers a way to interact and ask questions of other parents who might be dealing with similar problems. Again, there are many options to choose from, and a simple search should give you many options, depending on your needs and the needs of your child. Below are a few special groups and what they do. These groups are particularly helpful if you have a child with special needs or a disability because you will definitely have even more concerns about your little ones, and these groups can provide a lot of helpful information.

PARENT TO PARENT PROGRAM: For those moments when you want to talk to another parent whose child has the same issues as yours, this is your program. Like a dating website, it matches you with another parent that has similar struggles so you can support and assist each other. http://www.p2pusa.org/

CPRC: Community Parent Resource Center is funded to help a high-need audience and work with children with disabilities from birth through to age 26. They help parents get involved and better assist in their child's growth and education.

PTI: There are about 100 Parent Training and Information centers in the United States, and they provide a plethora of services for kids with disabilities, showing them what other groups and organizations exist that can help them better assist their child. https://www.parentcenterhub.org/find-your-center

NATIONAL FEDERATION OF FAMILIES: If you have a child that suffers from mental health issues, behavioral issues, emotional problems, or substance abuse problems, this national group has more than 120 chapters and state organizations that can help you with the

difficulties   you   might   be   facing.
https://www.ffcmh.org/resources

NAMI: The National Alliance for the Mentally Ill is yet another nationwide group that offers free peer support for people that suffer from mental health problems and supplies assistance and information that can help your family. https://www.nami.org/Home

AACAP: The American Academy of Child and Adolescent Psychiatry offers you fact sheets for parents and caregivers in both Spanish and English. It can assist you in locating information on adolescent and child psychiatry. https://www.aacap.org/

AAP: The American Academy of Pediatrics offers a family-friendly website which is called Healthy Children. Here you will be able to find so much information in Spanish and in English about different emotional problems your   children   might   suffer   from.
https://www.healthychildren.org/English/health-issues/conditions/emotional-problems/Pages/default.aspx

If you are having problems with your child, and you need medical help but do not have insurance, you can find out what your state's policies are, what is covered by them, and how to put in an application by calling 1.877.543.7669 or you can look at https://www.insurekidsnow.gov/

If you have reached a point where you are thinking you just can't take it anymore, don't give up! Because there is definitely support out there! You can get a helping hand from therapy, and deciding to go see a counselor is not admitting defeat but accepting an assist from someone with the one thing you definitely do not have—a step back advantage and training. There is absolutely no shame in asking for help, and the wisest people know when they need it.

Actually, asking for support shows you truly want to be the best parent you can. You can go to therapy on your own, with one child, with your partner, or with your entire family. This will depend on the problems you face and what will best fix them. This is the place for you to find the support and guidance you need to be a better parent. In this safe space, you can talk out any and all of your issues, from everyday annoyances and how to deal with them to more serious issues like postpartum depression or spousal abuse. In this way, seeking help will not only be beneficial to you, but also to your entire family.

But how do you know if you need to go to therapy? Almost everyone I know is in therapy these days for one thing or another, so going to talk to someone because you are an angry parent is nothing out of the ordinary. Being a parent is a rough job, and it is one that is guaranteed to raise you stress levels, make you lose sleep, cause you to make less healthy lifestyle choices (when you are too tired to cook so you order in Chinese or you just can't make it to the gym because you have to take one child to gymnastics and another to swim class), but all of these things make you less likely to do a good job as a parent and make you more likely to lose your temper. Not everyone needs therapy, and it is up to you to decide if you have reached that point. Maybe you have a wonderful support system in your family and friends who can help you out when you are anxious or stressed or need a moment to yourself, and, if so, lucky you! However, if you don't have any assistance and think you might be suffering from something more serious like postpartum depression or maybe post-traumatic stress disorder, these things will definitely keep you from being the best parent you can be, so it might be time to reach out for help.

Signs You May Need to See a Therapist:

— Depression

— Chronic anxiety

— Uncontrollable anger

— Chronic worry

— Irritability

— Uncontrollable crying

— (PTSD) Post-traumatic stress disorder

— Mood swings

— Manic episodes

— (OCD) Obsessive compulsive disorder

— Sexual disorders

— Phobias

— Eating disorders like anorexia or bulimia

If you or your child has gone through a serious trauma such as the loss of a pet, the death of a friend or a family member, maybe you have recently moved, or lost your home, suffered domestic abuse or rape, then these are things that can also warrant some time with a licensed therapist. You would not want your children to suffer from any of your past traumas, and therapy can help you make sure you don't do that.

There are also a bunch of things that you might run into, just life things, that throw you for a loop, making it difficult to be a good parent, but it is not something you can handle coming back from alone. If you are having financial issues, or you lost your job, you had to move, you have a child that is having difficulty in school either with grades or a bully or with their so called friends, you are suffering from addictions of any kind, you are fighting with your partner, there was a death in the family, you are trying to arrange for childcare, you are arguing with an ex about child care, you might be adopting a child, someone in your family has gotten seriously ill—any of these things can push you to need someone to talk to. Do not struggle on your own when there is so much help out there. The longer you keep shoving negative things down inside, the worse it will be for you or your child when, inevitably, they resurface and you blow up like Mount Vesuvius.

When and if you decide to go see a therapist, you can approach it like you are hiring a babysitter. Before you go for a session, ask for references and follow up on them, and interview a few until you find someone you feel comfortable talking to and feel you can be open and honest with. Here are a few things you can ask any of your potential therapists:

● Can you tell me how long you have been practicing therapy?

● Can you tell me how much experience you have working with children and families?

● Can you tell me what I can expect from a typical session?

● Can you tell me what you specialize in?

● Can you tell me what experience you have dealing with the types of issues I am having?

● Can you tell me how many sessions you'd

recommend for my treatment?

● Can you please give me a few references?

● During my therapy would my children or partner be required to attend?

Most importantly, you want someone you will feel comfortable talking to and sharing all of your problems and fears and worries with. If you are wondering what a session might be like, obviously ask them during your interview. These days therapists generally use a variety of different methods, but the most common is simply talk therapy, a conversation between the two of you. They might also have you practice communication exercises so you can improve your ability to speak to your child, especially during disciplinary moments.

Roleplay is another fun exercise that helps you put yourself in your children's shoes, and you might have to pretend you are your child for a moment being told to clean their room by an angry parent! Another method, reframing, is a very helpful way to look at a feeling or a situation from another angle, for example they might teach you to tell your children something is a challenge instead of a problem, and with that simple redefinition, or reframing, of the word problem, you have now made it an exciting activity to complete or solve. Basically, you are teaching yourself to change the way you or your children look at things.

The reason I got my degree in psychology was to see what the heck was going on within my mind and also to analyze my entire family. I knew there were so many things wrong there, and the main issue revolved around my mother's constant anger. Therapy was not something that was offered as a resource when I was a kid, but it is one I have taken full advantage of as an adult. My mother needs to see a therapist because she holds onto so much hate and resentment and never lets it go, and I mean never, to the point that any little thing can set her over the edge. Recently, she yelled at me because, unbeknownst to me, I used to spit up on her when I was a baby. I am in my late 40s now.

The fact that an 80 year old woman would yell at me for something I did when I was an infant is preposterous, but it happened. Standing in the driveway, when I was about to leave, and probably not see her for another year, she chose that moment to scream at me about this. Obviously, there is a lot more going on in her than just anger. She simply chooses to express all of her feelings as anger, which is a problem for everyone who comes into contact with her. Remember, we talked about identifying the actual emotion your child was feeling, the "what" behind the anger. This is so important! If you can teach a child to do that, imagine the healthy adult they will grow into. My mother still needs to learn this, but you can't talk to her about feelings. Yet another thing we have discussed which is so important! Basically, you need to use my mother as a textbook for what not to do. She is an extreme case of what holding onto anger looks like, and the reason I am so fascinated by the subject.

I remember the night she started yelling at us because we were laughing at the dinner table. What happens when you tell children to stop laughing? Of course, they laugh even harder! She banished me to the formal dining room and my brother to the lounge and allowed my sister to stay at the kitchen table. To this day, I can still see my reflection in the gilded mirror across the room, the golden light from the chandelier illuminating my solitude as I sat formally alone at a table for ten. I looked up and I laughed. Then, I heard my brother start to laugh in the lounge and my sister start to laugh in the kitchen. My mother was not laughing, she was yelling, but wouldn't it have been so much better if she had just started to laugh along with us? Hopefully, you still have time to change your parenting style from one of anger to one of joy, and if anything I have said in this book has helped you, then my work is done.

I just don't want any child to grow up in a toxic environment, fearing their parents, not feeling like they can talk to them about anything, hiding in their rooms in the hopes they will be left alone and not yelled at for one thing or another. Celebrate your children and enjoy the time you have with them because, before you know it, they will be all grown up and gone from home. I can go a decade without talking to my mother simply because she has the uncanny ability to always make me feel bad. I don't think that's what you want your child to feel about you! Take the time to open those lines of healthy communication with them. Spend more time praising their accomplishments and helpful moments than you do barking at them about the negative things. Thank them for doing their chores, putting away the dishes when the dishwasher is clean, or keeping their room tidy. Even if that is what they are supposed to do, reinforce it with love and praise and attention. If you do lose your temper and yell, talk to them about it, apologize for losing your cool, and explain why you did.

Remember, it is your job to lead by example and show them how to properly express their feelings when they are upset. If you can't do it, how are you going to expect them to? Get to the root of their outbursts and yours and keep that anger journal until you know what triggers the steam to emerge from your ears. Once you know, try and avoid those triggers! Keep those snacks and something to drink in your bag, so nobody is crying because they are hungry or thirsty, and that goes for you and your child. We all get hangry sometimes!

Chapter Summary

- We learned it is more than okay to seek help when you are feeling overwhelmed as a parent.
- There are so many types of help available out there, such as parenting groups and classes.
- We learned what signs to look out for that we need to bring in professional help.

Conclusion

The fact that you have read this book shows you are taking decisive action to become a better parent and manage any anger you might experience within the years of child rearing. We have touched on many topics, from the reason your child might get angry, to the types of anger you can experience. You now know that carrying around anger or releasing it incorrectly can have negative effects on you and your children. This book has furnished you with tips on how to deal with your anger and how to handle your child's anger. You are aware of the importance of developing your emotional intelligence or your EQ, and we've shown you how you can better raise that level within yourself and your children.

We also discussed the things you should do for yourself, those moments of self-care time, and how important that is to your sanity. Carve out small spaces in your routine for self-care, create time for you, no matter how brief they might be. You will come back recharged and ready to be the calm, caring parent you truly want to be once again. This book has discussed the fact that there are different types of parenting styles, and you can determine which one you are currently using and what you can try if it is not working. Then we discussed the wonders of positive parenting and how you too can be this type of parent.

One of the most important things to take away from this book is how communication affects your relationship with your children. How you speak to your kids makes a world of difference! If you want to strengthen your relationship with your little one, the easiest thing to do is talk to them, every day, with love and with genuine interest. Please take the time to make them feel special! Show them that their thoughts and opinions matter to you! If you can develop and maintain a healthy line of communication with your child, then there is really nothing you can't tackle as they grow up. It's only when those lines of communication get corrupted, when you yell and scream, when they talk back flippantly, that you have to rebuild those roads, dig them up and repave them. Take this time to set down something smooth and comfortable for everyone in your family to travel on.

If you have passed a point where you think you can fix the problems you face with your children alone, do not worry. There is so much help out there nowadays. You just have to ask for it and agree to utilize things like parenting groups, therapy, or parenting classes. These days, there are so many resources online, if you have a question, the answer is generally only a few clicks away. As long as you have access to a computer, you can easily find the solution to any specific problem you might have about your child. Our parents did not have the internet as a resource, so use it to your advantage.

Look, we all want to be the best parent for our child, and that starts with a happy, calm adult who can approach any situation rationally without resorting to falling into a fit of anger. We have to lead by example! That much is true. If you yell at your kids, they will yell back at you, and the cycle of anger will simply persist and carry on. Stop it in its tracks! This book has given you the tools to discipline and communicate with your child without getting upset, and now it is time to get back in the ring and become the parent you always wanted. You deserve to have the healthy relationship with your children that you wished you had had with your parents. I know I have a brilliant relationship with my little one, but it took time and energy and dedication, and I still have off days. But I want you to reach the stage I have, where the heart days fill your calendar almost completely, and let me just say it is truly a magical thing! If I can do it, you can do it too. If this book has helped you and you enjoyed and learned something, please be kind enough to review us on Amazon.

References

1. Vassar, Gerry & Wagenhals, Diane (2004) "Understanding Anger" Lakeside Educational Network accessed on 12/20/21
https://lakesidelink.com/blog/lakeside/how-does-a-parents-anger-impact-his-or-her-child/

2. Markham Ph.D., Laura, "How to Handle Your Anger at Your Child" Psychology Today

3. "75 Causes of Anger in Children," The Helpful Counselor
https://www.thehelpfulcounselor.com

4. "Ages & Stages: Understanding Children's Anger," Early Childhood Today, Scholastic

5. Morin, Amy, (2021, October 17)."7 Ways to Help a Child Cope With Anger," LCSW
accessed on 12722721
https://www.verywellfamily.com/ways-to-help-an-angry-child-1094976

6. "What Is Child Psychology and Why Is It Important?" Western Washington Medical Group
https://www.wwmedgroup.com/blog/child-psychology/

7. Gilles LCPC, Gary, "How to be an Emotionally Intelligent Parent – Part I" MentalHealth.Net, accessed on 12723721
https://www.mentalhelp.net/blogs/how-to-be-an-emotionally-intelligent-parent-part-i/

8. Pelini Ph.D, Sanya, (2020, May 11). "5 Things Emotionally Intelligent Parents Don't Do, Raising

Emotionally Intelligent Kids Starts with Emotionally Intelligent Parents," Health + Development/Mental Health, accessed on 12/24/21

https://www.parentmap.com/article/5-things-emotionally-intelligent-parents-dont-do

9. "Self-Care Inventory,"National Alliance on Mental Illness, Retrieved from nami.org: accessed on 12/25/21

https://www.nami.org/getattachment/Extranet/Educ ation,-Training-and-Outreach-Programs/Signature-Classes/NAMI-Homefront/HF-Additional-Resources/HF15AR6SelfCare.pdf.

10. Morin, Amy, LCSW (2020, January 31). "15 Self-Care Strategies for Parents, Simple but Effective Ways to Take Care of Yourself," Very Well Family, accessed on 12/26/21

https://www.verywellfamily.com/self-care-for-parents-4178010

11. (2019, May 20). "How to Teach Your Children About Self Care," Community Access Network, accessed on 12/27/21

https://www.communityaccessnetwork.org/how-to-teach-your-children-about-self-care/

12. (2021, September 16). "What is My Parenting Style: Four Types of Parenting," Bright Horizons accessed on 12/28/21

https://www.brighthorizons.com/family-resources/parenting-style-four-types-of-parenting

13. Morin, Amy, LCSW (2021, October 9). "4 Types of Parenting Styles and Their Effects on Kids -What's Your Parenting Style?" accessed on 12/29/21

https://www.verywellfamily.com/types-of-parenting-styles-1095045

14. "Positive Parenting Tips," Centers for Disease Control and Prevention accessed on 12/30/21

https://www.cdc.gov/ncbddd/childdevelopment/positive parenting/index.html

15. Harvey, Barbara, "Positive Parenting Defined," Kars4KidsParenting

https://parenting.kars4kids.org/positive-parenting-defined/

16. Legal Dictionary, Parenting Classes accessed on 12/30/21

https://legaldictionary.net/parenting-classes/

17. (2018, October). Center for Parent Information & Resources, accessed on 12/31/21

https://www.parentcenterhub.org/parentgroups/

18. Bradley, Sarah, (2021, August 22), "Help Point Your Children in the Right Direction," Best Online Parenting Classes

https://www.verywellfamily.com/best-online-parenting-classes-4845080

19. Langham, Ph.D., Dr. R.Y., (2018, April 2). Parenting Counseling, TherapyTribe Find Wellness accessed on 01/01/22

https://www.therapytribe.com/therapy/parenting-therapy/

20- (2020, August 31).The Australian Parenting Website, Raisingchildren.net.au, accessed 01/02/22
https://raisingchildren.net.au/toddlers/connecting-communicating/communicating/communicating-well-with-children